THE IMPORTANCE OF

Anne Frank

These and other titles are included in The Importance Of
biography series:

Anne Frank

by
John F. Wukovits

Lucent Books, P.O. Box 289011, San Diego, CA 92198-9011

Library of Congress Cataloging-in-Publication Data

Wukovits, John F., 1944–
    Anne Frank / by John F. Wukovits.
       p.   cm.—(The importance of)
    Includes bibliographical references and index.
    Summary: Discusses the life of Anne Frank, focusing on
the years she and her family spent in hiding and the impact
of her story upon the world.
    ISBN 1-56006-353-X (lib. : alk. paper)
    1. Frank, Anne, 1929–1945—Juvenile literature.   2. Jewish
children in the Holocaust—Netherlands—Amsterdam—
Biography—Juvenile literature.   3. Jews—Netherlands—
Amsterdam—Biography—Juvenile literature.   4. Holocaust,
Jewish (1939–1945)—Netherlands—Juvenile literature.
5. Amsterdam (Netherlands)—Biography—Juvenile literature.
[1. Frank, Anne, 1929–1945.   2. Jews—Netherlands—
Biography.   3. Holocaust, Jewish (1939–1945)—Netherlands
—Amsterdam.   4. Women—Biography.]   I. Title.   II. Series.
DS135.N6F739   1999
940.53'18'092—dc21   98–4327
    [B]   CIP
                                                                                        AC

Contents

Foreword

THE IMPORTANCE OF biography series deals with individuals who have made a unique contribution to history. The editors of the series have deliberately chosen to cast a wide net and include people from all fields of endeavor. Individuals from politics, music, art, literature, philosophy, science, sports, and religion are all represented. In addition, the editors did not restrict the series to individuals whose accomplishments have helped change the course of history. Of necessity, this criterion would have eliminated many whose contribution was great, though limited. Charles Darwin, for example, was responsible for radically altering the scientific view of the natural history of the world. His achievements continue to impact the study of science today. Others, such as Chief Joseph of the Nez Percé, played a pivotal role in the history of their own people. While Joseph's influence does not extend much beyond the Nez Percé, his nonviolent resistance to white expansion and his continuing role in protecting his tribe and his homeland remain an inspiration to all.

These biographies are more than factual chronicles. Each volume attempts to emphasize an individual's contributions both in his or her own time and for posterity. For example, the voyages of Christopher Columbus opened the way to European colonization of the New World. Unquestionably, his encounter with the New World brought monumental changes to both Europe and the Americas in his day. Today, however, the broader impact of Columbus's voyages is being critically scrutinized. *Christopher Columbus,* as well as every biography in The Importance Of series, includes and evaluates the most recent scholarship available on each subject.

Each author includes a wide variety of primary and secondary source quotations to document and substantiate his or her work. All quotes are footnoted to show readers exactly how and where biographers derive their information, as well as provide stepping stones to further research. These quotations enliven the text by giving readers eyewitness views of the life and times of each individual covered in The Importance Of series.

Finally, each volume is enhanced by photographs, bibliographies, chronologies, and comprehensive indexes. For both the casual reader and the student engaged in research, The Importance Of biographies will be a fascinating adventure into the lives of people who have helped shape humanity's past and present, and who will continue to shape its future.

IMPORTANT DATES IN THE LIFE OF ANNE FRANK

1929

Anneliese Marie Frank is born in Frankfurt, Germany, on June 12.

1933

Adolf Hitler becomes Germany's leader; the first edicts restricting the rights of Jews are implemented; the first concentration camp opens; Otto Frank travels to Amsterdam to locate a home outside Germany for his family.

1939

Germany attacks Poland on September 1 and begins World War II.

1940

The German army quickly defeats the Dutch army and marches into Amsterdam. The Franks are trapped.

1942

Anne receives a diary for her thirteenth birthday; the Franks go into hiding in the Secret Annex.

1944

June 6, the Allied armies launch the long-awaited invasion of Europe, lifting the spirits of the eight people confined in the Annex; August, the eight are arrested and sent to Westerbork; September, the Franks are shipped to the death camps at Auschwitz-Birkenau in Poland, and Mr. van Pels is executed at Auschwitz; October, Anne and Margot are transferred to Bergen-Belsen in Germany; December, Friedrich Pfeffer dies in Neuengamme concentration camp.

1945

Edith Frank dies at Auschwitz; Mrs. van Pels dies in Theresienstadt concentration camp; Margot Frank dies of typhus at Bergen-Belsen; Anne Frank dies of typhus in Bergen-Belsen; Peter van Pels dies in Mauthausen concentration camp; Otto Frank, the only survivor from the Annex, returns to Amsterdam and is given Anne's diary; World War II ends.

1947

Titled *Het Achterhuis*, Anne's diary is published in Amsterdam.

1950

Anne's diary is published in Germany.

1952

Titled *Anne Frank: The Diary of a Young Girl*, Anne's diary is published in England and the United States.

1955

The Diary of Anne Frank, a play based on Anne's diary opens in New York City and wins the Tony Award for best drama.

1956

The play wins the Pulitzer Prize in drama.

1980

Otto Frank dies in Switzerland.

The Life of Anne Frank

Anne Frank is one of the most celebrated teenagers in world history. Schoolchildren learn how the German Jewish girl and her family were hidden by Dutch friends during the Nazi occupation of Holland, only to be captured and sent to concentration camps months before the end of World War II.

Plays present live depictions of the touching ordeal faced by Anne and her family; her diary is offered by youth book clubs. Teachers tell of a heroic individual who faced horrendous times with courage and inspiration, but they also speak about a vibrant youth whose dreams serve as a beacon to guide

A statue of Anne Frank stands in the Dutch city of Utrecht. Anne has become a symbol of heroism, and her diary remains a testament to the Holocaust.

other teenagers in search of their own uniqueness and whose finest characteristics make her a fitting role model.

That is as it should be, for Anne Frank deserves all the acclaim heaped upon her. However, most people rely almost entirely on her diary for information and, while the diary certainly tells a moving story that challenges many beliefs and prejudices, readers of this book alone by no means learn the full tale of its remarkable author. The diary covers only a brief portion of her fifteen incredible years—from June 12, 1942, until the first day of August 1944, when the entries suddenly stop. This inspirational teenager lived an extraordinary life before and after the period she wrote about, and these are the portions that most readers miss.

A surprisingly small number of books depicting Anne Frank's ordeal have appeared since her death in 1945 and, of those, few provide details of the younger Anne Frank or of her incarceration in different concentration camps. Without absorbing this information, the reader will not grasp the entire personality that comprises Anne. Heroic? Yes, but Anne was also a normal young girl with emotions and interests that swirled about every other girl of her day. The exuberance and charm for which she is famous were balanced with frivolity and anger, with petty school yard quarrels, with jealousy and short-temperedness. Thus it is important that readers receive a glimpse of the younger Anne Frank.

Without learning of Anne's time in German concentration camps, the reader will not comprehend the devastating effects of the Holocaust on the young girl, for it is by seeing Anne in those desolate

Anne's Names' Real Names

Other than for her own family members, Anne Frank changed the names of most people she mentioned in her diary. While she barely camouflaged some, such as those she gave the van Pels family, she altered others so that few could guess their identities.

Name Anne Used in Her Diary	Real Name
Miep van Santen	Hermine "Miep" Gies
Henk van Santen	Jan Gies
Hermann van Daan	Hermann van Pels
Petronella van Daan	Auguste van Pels
Peter van Daan	Peter van Pels
Albert Dussel	Friedrich "Fritz" Pfeffer
Victor Kraler	Victor Kugler
Jo Koophuis	Johannes Kleiman
Elli Vossens	Bep Voskuijl
Lies Goosens	Hannah Elisabeth Pick-Goslar

surroundings that one discerns the changes in her personality. The creative, cheerful individual who was captured by the Nazis was transformed into a scared young girl who wanted to live, but because her body was weakened by disease and near starvation, succumbed to death only weeks before she would have been liberated. This is the portion of her life that most accounts ignore.

The Importance of Anne Frank

Anne Frank has inspired people over the past half-century, and her story will continue to move readers as long as books survive and people can read. She did not suffer alone in the Holocaust. Millions of other people, Jewish and non-Jewish, endured pain, separation, confinement, and death, but their tales remain buried in anonymity. The vast majority of those people suffered in silence, and their stories died with them. They have no one to speak for them—except Anne. Her story typifies the ordeals faced by men, women, and especially children of those years, and thus it is important that it reach the largest number of people.

Anne Frank's story fills another great need for mankind. Since the end of World War II various neo-Nazi and other hate groups have denied that the Holocaust ever happened. They claim that the entire episode was fabricated by individuals who hope to destroy Adolf Hitler's reputation. Anne Frank stands as a powerful answer to these groups and as such helps to prevent the occurrence of another Holocaust.

1 "They Had Simply Closed the Door of Their Lives"

The teenage girl awoke with a start to her mother's anxious summons to get out of bed and gather her belongings. Anne Frank had slept soundly, and awakening at 5:30 A.M. was neither a familiar nor a welcome occurrence, but the spring of 1942 was an unusual time. She and the rest of her family—her father, Otto; her mother, Edith; and her older sister, Margot—were rushing into hiding, for they were Jews living in a nation occupied by Nazi troops, brutal representatives of the fascist government of Germany, which had made killing Jews a matter of policy.

Conditions Deteriorate for Jews

On May 14, 1940, Anne's adopted country, Holland, had surrendered to Adolf Hitler's invading army. Soon her freedoms had begun to disappear in a harsh series of anti-Jewish measures. A close family friend, Miep Gies, observed that the perilous times produced enormous anxiety. She noticed that Jews "whispered among themselves, then stopped whispering when people came near. They were suspicious always, and always now with downcast eyes. I felt an ache for these demoralized people when-

ever I saw them." Miep continued that the laws changed so frequently for Jewish families that, "Being Jewish had to feel these days as though one were standing on shifting sands—and for some, quicksand."[1]

Margot Must Report

The quicksand started to envelop Anne and her family on Monday, June 29, 1942, when an ominous announcement appeared in every Dutch newspaper that all Jews would be removed from their homes and transported to labor camps inside Germany. On Saturday of the same week, July 4, the Nazi authorities, speaking through an agency they had created, the Central Office for Jewish Emigration, issued an alarming batch of notices. Directed at a thousand Jewish teenagers between the ages of fifteen and eighteen, the notices contained orders for the recipients to appear on Monday for shipment out of the country. On this list was the name of Anne's older sister, Margot.

Sunday, July 5, started out in grand fashion for Anne, who lay on the balcony and enjoyed the sun's relaxing warmth with a boyfriend from school, sixteen-year-old Hello Silberberg. They chatted pleasantly about the usual topics that interest

Deportations in the Netherlands

Large-scale efforts to remove Jews from the Netherlands started within a year of the Nazi takeover of the country. In The War Against the Jews, 1933–1945, *Lucy S. Dawidowicz explains the timetable for "cleansing" the Netherlands of Jews.*

"In January 1942 forced-labor camps for Jews were set up. Meanwhile the Dutch Jews began to be concentrated in Amsterdam. On April 29, 1942, the identifying Jewish star was introduced. Jews were further restricted in their occupational activities. Curfew was introduced.

In July 1942, deportations began, continuing through September 1943. Two transit camps, Westerbork and Vught, were set up where Jews were concentrated until schedules permitted their entrainment to Auschwitz. . . .

Some 110,000 Jews were deported to Auschwitz, Sobibor, and, in smaller numbers, to other camps."

teenagers—school, friends, each other. Hello left after a while but told Anne he would return around 3:00 P.M.

Anne continued to luxuriate in the sun. Shortly before Hello was to return, Anne heard someone yell from outside their front door but dismissed the sounds as unimportant. Below, however, the drama had started to unfold. An officer, part of the Nazi-controlled Green Police, had arrived and handed over Margot's notice. When Margot stepped out onto the balcony, Anne knew something bad had happened, for a worried look blanketed her sister's face. Margot sat next to Anne and, in an attempt to avoid worrying her younger sister about what could soon occur to Anne, announced that their father had just been ordered to report to German authorities and that their mother had gone to some friends for help.

Anne later wrote, "I was stunned. A call up: everyone knows what that means. Visions of concentration camps and lonely cells raced through my head."[2]

Before Anne had time to fully comprehend the news, she heard another knock at the door. Her boyfriend had appeared as promised. By now her mother had returned with a family friend, Mr. Hermann van Pels, and Anne could hear her mother saying something to Hello. After a moment, Hello left. Margot then informed Anne that instead of their father, it was she who had received the call-up notice.

"At this second shock, I began to cry," recalled Anne, and the entire household erupted in fear and panic.[3]

Preparations to Leave

A degree of calm settled in when Anne's father, Otto, arrived around 5:00 P.M. Immediately he contacted an associate,

The rear of the building in which Otto Frank ran his business. Here, Otto prepared a secret hiding place for his family in some spare rooms behind his office.

business offices, some startling information. "Miep, I have a secret to confide to you. Miep, Edith, Margot, Anne, and I are planning to go under—to go into hiding." While the concerned secretary absorbed this information, Mr. Frank added that the van Pelses would join them, and the seven people intended to move into some old rooms located near the back of Otto's business that had once been used to conduct pharmacy experiments.

Otto Frank then arrived at the key portion of what he had to say. "As you will be working on, as usual, right next to us, I need to know if you have any objections?" Mr. Frank fully understood that his intention to hide in the building placed his friends in jeopardy, for non-Jews accused of assisting Jews in fleeing from the Nazis were routinely arrested and placed in concentration camps.

Without hesitation, Miep replied she had no objections. To emphasize the seriousness of their situation and to give Miep another opportunity to back away, Mr. Frank added, "Miep, are you willing to take on the responsibility of taking care of us while we are in hiding?"

Again without pause, Miep replied, "Of course."

Otto Frank stared at his friend with a look of relief and gratitude. "Miep, for those who help Jews, the punishment is harsh; imprisonment, perhaps—"

Miep cut him off before he could add anything worse. "I said, 'Of course.' I meant it." Miep then "asked no further questions. The less I knew, the less I could say in an interrogation."[4]

For months Mr. Frank and a small circle of collaborators, including Miep and Jan, had been carefully cleaning up a back addition to his business office and had

Victor Kugler, while Mr. van Pels rushed out to bring back two other non-Jewish friends, Miep and Jan Gies.

Though he did not know exactly when it would arrive, Otto had foreseen this day and had begun preparing a hiding place for his family. One day he mentioned to Miep, who worked as a secretary in his cautiously begun moving in boxes of household items and pieces of furniture. Though he had originally planned to take his family into hiding in mid-July, Margot's call-up notice forced him to move instantly, for once she failed to appear as ordered, police would rush to the family's home to arrest everyone.

Miep and Jan Help

That Sunday evening Mr. van Pels rang the bell to Miep and Jan's apartment. The two understood how unusual it was for someone to be outside after dark during wartime, so the "tension rose in the apartment at the sound. Our eyes darted from one to another." Jan cautiously opened the door to find their friend "in quite an agitated condition."

Mr. van Pels muttered in a low, nervous voice, "Come right away. Margot Frank has received a postcard ordering her to appear for forced-labor shipment to Germany. She's been ordered to bring a suitcase with winter things. The Franks have decided to go immediately into hiding. Can you come right now to take a few things they'll need in hiding?"[5] The Dutch couple quickly agreed.

Miep and Jan hurried to their friends' apartment to begin transporting bags of clothing to the hiding place. The sense of terror was so pervasive that Miep recalled, "I could feel their urgency, an undercurrent of near-panic," for everyone knew the Franks had to flee before the following afternoon, when the Germans might begin searching for Margot. Miep's heart especially went out to Anne, whose eyes were so wide that they reminded Miep of "saucers, a mixture of excitement and terrible fright."[6]

Hiding the Jews

In her book, The Holocaust: The Destruction of European Jewry, *Nora Levin describes some of the difficulties faced by Jews who tried to go into hiding in the Netherlands.*

"Not only did the crushing power of the Nazis in Holland destroy Jews; the geography of the country also conspired against them. Holland is flat, and apart from marshlands in the coastal regions, there are no woods or hiding places. It is also a very small country, making it hard for anyone to submerge. Moreover, there were no exits during the Nazi occupation. On the east was the Reich; to the south was occupied Belgium; and on the west and north, the open sea. . . . But in the teeth of these immense difficulties, Dutch Christians made thousands of heroic efforts to save Jews and hide them in attics, ceiling spaces and cellars, in private homes, cloisters and orphanages."

Extreme care had to be taken to avoid arousing suspicion. The occupying Germans offered rewards to anyone who delivered information about Jews in hiding, and Miep and Jan understood that if they were caught helping their friends, they could also end up in a concentration camp. To make matters worse, the Frank family had rented an upstairs room to a divorced man in his thirties named Goldschmidt. Though the tenant was also Jewish, Anne's father wanted him to know as little as possible. Thus, even inside the relative safety of their own home, they had to be careful.

"With our coats bursting, Jan and I made our way back to our rooms and quickly unloaded what we'd had under our coats," Miep later wrote. "We put it all under our bed. Then, our coats empty again, we hurried back to [Anne's house] to get another load."[7] After retrieving a second batch of clothes, Miep and Jan departed at 11:30 P.M. An exhausted Anne climbed into bed and "even though I knew it'd be my last night in my own bed, I fell asleep right away."[8]

Monday, July 6, 1942

Her mother's 5:30 A.M. call brought Anne back to reality, for she had to quickly decide what to pack into one schoolbag and one satchel. Each item carried its own memories for Anne, and leaving any behind was like severing a small, yet important, part of her past from her present. "The first thing I stuck in was this diary, and then curlers, handkerchiefs, schoolbooks, a comb and some old letters," she wrote. While wondering if she had been

practical, Anne knew that if she were to be in hiding for an indefinite period of time, cut off from all she knew and loved, she would need something to remind her of the good days. "Memories mean more to me than dresses," she explained.[9]

At 7:30 A.M. on a dreary, rainy Monday, Miep arrived on her bicycle to begin moving the family into hiding. As planned by Anne's father, Miep and Margot would ride ahead, followed a bit later by Anne and her parents, walking. As soon as Miep arrived, Margot, wearing many layers of clothing, rushed out the door and retrieved her bicycle, which she had kept despite a law forbidding Jews to own such means of personal transporta-

Miep Gies bravely aided the Frank family while they were in hiding.

Why Some Helped

In Milton Meltzer's Rescue: The Story of How Gentiles Saved Jews in the Holocaust, *Johtje Vos explains why she helped hide Jews during the Nazi occupation.*

"Well, my husband and I never sat down and discussed it or said, 'Let's go and help some Jews.' It happened. It was a spontaneous reaction, actually. Such things, such responses depend on fate, on the result of your upbringing, your character, on your general love for people, and most of all, on your love for God. And, I would say, there was also a kind of nonchalance and optimism about it. I would say to myself, 'Oh come on, you can do that.'"

tion. The senior Franks silently looked toward Miep as they entrusted their older daughter to her care, but Miep tried to reassure them that all would be well. "Don't worry," she told the parents. "The rain is very heavy. Even the Green Police won't want to go out in it."

Miep peered toward Margot then, hoping to look like typical Dutch women on their way to work, the two began their casual ride away from the Frank family's home. As Miep edged down the street she glanced back at Anne, who gazed out from the doorway "wide-eyed in a nightgown."

Danger lurked on each corner and on every street, for by now other people had started to appear. The two riders continued without conversation, and though they spotted no Green Police in the bad weather, they could not relax. As Miep recalled, "We both knew that from the moment we'd mounted our bicycles we'd become criminals. There we were, a Christian and a Jew without the yellow star, riding on an illegal bicycle." Margot was a fugitive from the law and Miep was her ac-

complice, but the two maintained their calm front. "Margot's face showed no intimidation," explained Miep. "She betrayed nothing of what she was feeling inside. Suddenly we'd become two allies against the might of the German beast among us."[10]

While Margot and Miep rode ahead, Anne and her parents prepared for their walk to the hiding place. They could not take large suitcases on the 2.5-mile journey to their destination, since two adults and a teenager carrying heavy luggage would be recognizable by anyone as a family of Jews attempting to leave. Anne's father decided that they would wear as many layers of clothing as possible, and that each one could bring along a small schoolbag and a satchel.

One by one, Anne donned an array of items: two vests, three pairs of pants, one dress, one skirt, a jacket, a pair of summer shorts, two pairs of stockings, heavy lace-up shoes, a woolly cap, a scarf, and other items. The more she could wear the better, because these clothes would have to last for a long time. Anne wrote that they were covered with so many layers of clothes that "it looked as if we were going off to spend the night in a refrigerator." Instead, they were heading into the humid warmth of July. "I was suffocating even before we left the house." [11]

Anne had no time to say goodbye to her friends, not even a moment to phone Hello and mutter a few tender words. However, she paused when she glanced at her cat Moortje. The thought of leaving her pet tore Anne's heart, for she and Moortje had formed a bond that would have been unbreakable in normal times. "Moortje, my cat, was the only living creature I said goodbye to," [12] Anne morosely wrote later.

Anne's father scribbled a note asking Mr. Goldschmidt to give Moortje to the neighbors. The three fugitives then picked up their satchels and schoolbags and headed into the rain. Anne took one last look at everything familiar and comfortable, then wheeled about and walked toward the alien world that was to be hers for the indeterminate future.

As the three proceeded down the sidewalk, Dutch citizens passing by extended sympathetic looks. Many Dutch non-Jews despised what the Germans were doing, but few would risk incarceration or death to lend a helping hand. The three struggled along, alone with their thoughts and fears as the rain fell.

Entering the Annex

In the meantime, Miep and Margot arrived at the hiding place and stored away their bicycles. Once safely inside, Margot's outward facade of bravery started to dissolve, and as Miep recalled, "I could see that Margot was suddenly on the verge of crumbling." Miep took Margot's arm and guided her to the entrance to the hiding place. "As she opened the door," wrote Miep, "I gripped her arm to give her courage. Still, we said nothing. She disappeared behind the door and I took my place in the front office." [13]

Not long after, Anne and her parents arrived, thoroughly soaked and exhausted from their walk. Miep led them through a long hallway and up a wooden staircase. Margot, who was waiting at the top of the stairs, stood awkwardly for a few seconds while the others absorbed their first glimpse of their makeshift home.

"The situation was very upsetting," explained Miep. "I wanted to leave the family alone together. I couldn't begin to imagine what they must be feeling to have walked away from everything they owned in the world—their home; a lifetime of gathered possessions; Anne's little cat, Moortje. Keepsakes from the past. And friends.

"They had simply closed the door of their lives and had vanished from Amsterdam." [14]

2 The Franks in Germany

Chapter

For centuries the Franks had been as typical a German family as one could find. Members spoke German, wore German outfits, celebrated German festivals, attended German schools, appreciated German music and art, and served in the German army. Family roots in Frankfurt, Germany, stretched back to the 1600s. For a U.S. citizen of European descent to claim such a lengthy lineage, the person's ancestors would have had to cross the Atlantic Ocean to America in the early 1700s—before the birth of George Washington, before the establishment of all the original colonies, and before the firing of the first shots in the French and Indian War.

The Franks Meet

Otto Frank, Anne's father, was born on May 12, 1889, in Frankfurt, the second son of Michael Frank and Alice Betty Stern. A clever businessman, Michael Frank not only owned and directed a German bank called the Bankgeschäft Michael, which he started in 1885, but he purchased part ownership in a travel agency and in companies that produced throat lozenges and cigars. As a result, his family members lived in comfort and enjoyed their large circle of

friends—both Jewish and non-Jewish—in Frankfurt, a town known for its open acceptance of various races and religions.

After graduating in 1908 from Frankfurt's Lessing Gymnasium (a European "gymnasium" is like a U.S. prep school), Otto Frank enrolled in the famous University of Heidelberg. He dropped out after one semester, however, to take advantage of a golden business opportunity. The family of one of his college friends, Nathan Straus, owned R. H. Macy, New York's largest department store. The pair headed across the Atlantic to learn the intricacies of operating a retail business by working in various positions in the famed establishment. Otto's father died the next year, however, and the young man returned to Germany.

When much of Europe erupted with the start of World War I in 1914, Otto enlisted in the army like any patriotic German. Commissioned as an officer in an artillery unit, he fought against French and British troops in France. When the war ended four years later, in a disastrous defeat for Germany, Otto was sent home from the army with the rank of lieutenant.

On May 12, 1925, the thirty-six-year-old Otto Frank married Edith Hollander, eleven years his junior, in Aachen, Germany, near the Dutch border. A member of

Otto Frank and his daughters were born in Frankfurt, Germany, a city that claimed the second largest population of Jews in the nation.

one of Aachen's most prominent families, Edith joined her husband for a delightful honeymoon in the sunny Mediterranean resorts of southern Italy. Afterward, the couple lived with Otto's mother for slightly more than two years.

Though Otto preferred other occupations to banking, someone had to take control of the Bankgeschäft Michael following the death of its founder. Thus Otto had joined the bank some two years before his marriage, but at the same time, he dabbled in other ventures. In 1923 he journeyed to Amsterdam, where he established his own banking and traveling company in collaboration with a Dutch citizen, Johannes Kleiman. However, the company lasted barely over a year before Otto closed its doors.

Starting a Family

On February 16, 1926, a little more than one year after their marriage, a jubilant Otto and Edith welcomed the first of their two daughters, Margot Betti Frank. A second daughter, Anneliese Marie Frank, was

born on June 12, 1929. To provide more space and privacy for the family, Otto purchased a new home on Marbachweg in Frankfurt, consisting of the first two floors of a house and complete with a garden. The Franks hoped to offer their girls more open spaces and a neighborhood filled with other children their age. Their dream came true, and before long, the garden resonated with the happy shouts and cheerful sounds of friends who came to play with young Margot and her baby sister, Anne.

The Franks constructed a pleasant childhood for their daughters. Frankfurt boasted a long history of tolerance toward all religions, so the town's thirty thousand Jews—the second largest concentration of Jews in Germany after the nation's capital, Berlin—felt secure among the half-million people that comprised Frankfurt's population in the 1920s. As Reform Jews, Otto and Edith raised their children to be proud of their Jewish heritage. They instilled values of openness and fair play into their daughters and taught them to treat each individual and every religious group with courtesy. Their childhood friends came from a variety of religious backgrounds—Catholic, Protestant, Jewish. It was commonplace for Margot or Anne to be invited to a first communion celebration or for the Franks to invite other children to observe Hanukkah.

Besides religious tolerance, Otto stressed a love for reading and thinking. A huge bookcase packed with books dominated one room in the home on Marbachweg. Most nights, Otto crafted intricate and delightful bedtime tales to spur his daughters to investigate new ideas and form their own opinions.

In March 1931 the family moved to a five-room apartment at number 24, Ganghoferstrasse, a Frankfurt neighborhood that offered lovely walking paths and choice hills that were perfectly suited for tobogganing in the winter. In short time, Margot romped through the area with her new friends, while the two-year-old Anne charged about the garden and its main attraction—a sandbox.

While the Franks settled into what appeared to be a promising lifetime as a happy family, there were ominous political rumblings that would soon threaten the Franks' peaceful existence. The disturbing sounds were caused by a man only three weeks older than Otto Frank—Adolf Hitler.

The Rise of Hitler

Born on April 20, 1889, in the small Austrian town of Braunau-am-Inn, Adolf Hitler was the fourth child of Klara and Alois Hitler. While Otto Frank traveled to New York to learn business, Hitler wandered about parts of Europe, often broke and homeless. The future dictator had dropped out of school at the age of sixteen to pursue his love of art, but his hopes were crushed in 1908 when the prestigious Vienna Arts Academy refused to admit him because he lacked sufficient artistic talent.

Events swirling about Europe altered Hitler's life. In 1914 World War I plunged Germany and Austria into battle against England and France, but it saved Hitler. He enrolled in the German army, where instead of being a vagrant and a beggar, he served with distinction as a dispatch runner, a soldier who delivered messages from commanding officers in the rear to soldiers fighting on the front lines. Often volunteering for hazardous missions that other runners declined, Hitler earned the Iron Cross, one of Germany's top medals for bravery.

Hitler loved serving in the military. However, on October 13, 1918, he was exposed to deadly chlorine gas, which killed some members of his unit and left Hitler blind and gasping for breath. He eventually recovered his sight, but before he could return to the front, Germany had surrendered, and the war was over. A distraught Hitler claimed that Germany's brave soldiers had been betrayed by politicians back home who should not have agreed to stop fighting.

Hitler's consternation did not diminish when he returned to Germany and learned about the Treaty of Versailles, whose harsh terms angered many other Germans, as well. Especially galling were the so-called guilt clauses, which the victorious nations, especially England and France, had imposed on the defeated country. For example, Germany was forced to accept blame for causing the war, and its citizens were required to pay for the monumental damage that had occurred in other countries. As German citizens experienced difficulty locating or purchasing food and shelter for themselves, they rebelled against this extra burden and castigated their diplomats and politicians for having given in so readily. The time was ripe for a charismatic leader to take advantage of the unrest and sweep to power.

Growing Anti-Semitism

At first Hitler remained in the army, where he was assigned to spy on different groups of Germans who might be a threat to the postwar government. One of the groups he investigated was the tiny German Workers' Party, which he joined in September 1919 as member #7. Within two years he had resigned from the army and risen to command of the party. Hitler, feasting on the people's dissatisfaction of the government and fomenting the hatred of Jews that historically had appeared when Europeans wanted a scapegoat, set in motion a chain of events that ended with the continent in ruins.

Anti-Semitism, which is a word that describes hatred of Jews, has existed for many centuries. Following the crucifixion of Jesus of Nazareth, Christians tried to convince others that Jesus was the Christ, the son of God. The majority of the Jewish people, however, refused to accept this belief, and a bitter reaction ensued. From the fourth century to the nineteenth century, an array of laws restricted the rights of Jews: Jews could not own property in many locations; they could not become lawyers, painters, or architects; Jews could not marry Christians. Occasionally, Christians destroyed Jewish holy books and even burned Jews at the stake.

To justify what were obviously horrendous acts, some Christians spread lies about the Jews. People claimed that Jews poisoned water wells and murdered babies. Some priests labeled Jews as friends of the devil who loved to steal and swindle others out of their money. Mostly, though, Christians accused Jews of being Christ-killers, for Jesus had been crucified in the Jewish land of ancient Palestine.

Adolf Hitler (far left) earned the Iron Cross for bravery during World War I. Hitler believed that Germany's weakened position after its surrender in the war was due in part to conspiring Jews.

Medieval priests delivered sermons bitterly attacking Jews. One of the Catholic Church's most revered early leaders, Father John Chrysostom, proclaimed in the fourth century, "Where Christ-killers gather, the cross is ridiculed, God blasphemed, the father unacknowledged, the son insulted, the grace of the Spirit rejected. . . . If the Jewish rites are holy and venerable, our way of life must be false. But if our way is true, as indeed it is, theirs is fraudulent."[15]

Igniting Destructiveness

As a result, periodic outbreaks of violence occurred against Jews through the centuries. While intervals existed during which conditions calmed and Jews lived relatively normal lives, anti-Semitism always lurked beneath the surface. It required only a dynamic individual like Hitler to ignite latent hatred into full-fledged destructiveness.

Sensing that his future lay in politics, Hitler resigned from the army to direct the German Workers' Party. A powerful speaker who moved crowds with his fiery rhetoric and hypnotic eyes, Hitler employed a combination of pride in the nation and anti-Semitism to enlarge the party ranks. His bitter attacks, which blamed Jews and communists for all Germany's problems, found a receptive audience. An August 1921 police report stated that "the mood for Jewish pogroms [organized assaults on a people] is spreading systematically in all parts of the country."[16]

Party membership increased dramatically, pumped up by disenchanted Germans, drawn by Hitler's promises of a better Germany. Hitler changed the organization's name to the National Socialist German Workers' Party, or Nazi after an abbreviated form of the first two German words, and adopted the swastika, or twisted cross, as a party symbol. A twenty-five-point program called

A 1922 photo of the newly formed National Socialist German Workers' Party. Hitler and the Nazi Party promised to restore pride to Germans who felt demoralized by harsh war reparations and the effects of the Great Depression.

for the exclusion of Jews from German society. By 1923 the party's ranks had grown from 1,000 to 150,000.

Buttressed by the swelling Nazi ranks, Hitler attempted to take over the national government on November 8, 1923, in an ill-fated putsch, or rebellion, in the south German city of Munich. Police quickly arrested Hitler, but the trial that followed brought him the acclaim he had sought. On trial for treason, which could have resulted in his execution, Hitler faced a sympathetic judge and prosecutors who permitted him to use the proceedings as a platform to publicize Nazi doctrine. Instead of a harsh sentence, Hitler received the lightest one possible under the law—five years in prison. The nine months he actually spent in jail, which he served in relative luxury and semifreedom, offered him the chance to express his spiteful views in a book titled *Mein Kampf* (*My Struggle*). Though few leaders in Germany or elsewhere in Europe took his writing seriously, in this book, Hitler stated that his objective was to run the country, and he outlined precisely what he intended to do when he achieved power.

Hitler did not have to wait long. Worldwide events shifted in his favor with the October 1929 stock market crash on Wall Street and the Great Depression that plagued many industrialized nations in the 1930s. Hitler seized on this opportunity and promised to bring jobs to the vast numbers of unemployed people. He vowed to return glory and honor to Germany. These campaign promises, combined with his blustery condemnation of the Jews, garnered such strong support in the 1930 German national election that the Nazis stood as the second most powerful party in the country.

In the next major election, two years later, Hitler's Nazis captured more than one-third of the national vote. Because his organization was now the most powerful party in Germany, on January 30, 1933, Hitler was named chancellor of Germany, the nation's second-most important job. He quickly took steps to seize even more control, and when President Paul von Hindenburg died in 1934, he assumed the powers of president as well, becoming, in effect, dictator of the nation.

Anti-Jewish Measures

Hitler speedily instituted the first of what would be numerous anti-Jewish measures. On April 1, 1933, he organized a boycott—an action in which people refuse to shop at certain stores—of Jewish businesses, and he forced thousands of Jews out of Germany's civil service, the government's administrative organization. Most non-Jewish Germans applauded the measures, and signs appeared along highways: "JEWS ENTER THIS PLACE AT THEIR RISK," or "WARNING TO PICKPOCKETS AND JEWS." Near one German town, government leaders posted a notice at a dangerous curve that read, "DRIVE CAREFULLY, SHARP CURVE—JEWS, 75 MILES AN HOUR!"[17] Synagogues were defaced by anti-Jewish slogans such as "JEW PIG" and "DIE JEW."

Disturbing events occurred even in Otto Frank's beloved Frankfurt. The Nazi Party received so many votes in the March 13, 1933, Frankfurt city election that an ecstatic throng of Nazi sympathizers rushed to city hall for a rousing celebration. "Heil Hitler! Heil Hitler! Down with the Jews!" shouted the elated Nazis, who then stormed into the town hall, raised the Nazi flag, and forced the mayor to resign in favor of a Nazi party member.[18] Throughout the entire evening, German police looked on in amusement rather than attempt to restore order.

Otto Frank watched events with growing alarm. Like typical parents concerned for the welfare of their children, Otto and Edith tried to shield their daughters from the disturbing actions directed toward Jews by telling them nothing.

However, in the spring of 1933, when Jewish children were forced to use school benches separate from the rest of the children, Otto began planning to leave the country. The future that awaited the Franks in Germany offered nothing but sadness and pain; possibly elsewhere he could raise his two little girls in happiness and peace. Otto's mother, Alice Frank-Stern, had already packed her belongings and fled across the German border to Switzerland, and other family members were contemplating similar moves.

Otto decided that the family would relocate to Holland's main city, Amsterdam, which had long been known for its religious tolerance. Jews had migrated to Holland to escape persecution in Spain during the Middle Ages and in the early 1600s; the Pilgrims had settled in the Low Lands before crossing the Atlantic to America. By 1933 nearly a hundred thousand Jews resided in Holland, earning for Amsterdam the label "Jerusalem of Europe."

Otto's decision to leave was made easier by the misfortunes of the family bank, which like many financial and industrial concerns had fallen on hard times during the Great Depression. The imminent closure of the Bankgeschäft Michael meant that Otto could freely seek out other business opportunities. A brother-in-law, Erich Elias, had opened in Switzerland a branch of Opetka-Werke, a company that produced pectin, a jelling substance used in making jams and jellies. Elias informed Otto Frank that the company planned to open another branch in Amsterdam and, with Elias's assistance, Otto received the job. It was an attractive position because of

Hitler's Anti-Semitism

Why did Hitler focus his hatred on Jews? Lucy S. Dawidowicz, in her book The War Against the Jews, 1933–1945, *explains the German leader's mind.*

"He believed that they were the source of all evil, misfortune, and tragedy, the single factor that, like some inexorable law of nature, explained the workings of the universe. The irregularities of war and famine, financial distress and sudden death, defeat and sinfulness—all could be explained by the presence of that single factor in the universe, a miscreation that disturbed the world's steady ascent toward well-being, affluence, success, victory. A savior was needed to come forth and slay the loathsome monster. In Hitler's obsessed mind, . . . the Jews were the demonic hosts whom he had been given a divine mission to destroy."

Hitler blamed most of Germany's ills on the Jews. Giving the German people a scapegoat for their problems boosted national pride and swelled Nazi ranks.

its relative proximity to Otto's home country, Germany, and besides, he had already established business contacts in Amsterdam from earlier ventures. Rather than fleeing to Switzerland or crossing to North America, as some family and friends were doing, Otto settled on Germany's neighboring nation, Holland. The decision would haunt him not many years later.

In the summer of 1933 Otto Frank took his family to Aachen to stay with Edith's mother, where they would remain until he had located a suitable home for the family in Amsterdam. Though saddened to be parting from his wife and two lovely daughters, Otto Frank was convinced that his actions were pulling his family out of harm's way and placing them into a happier environment.

Otto Frank did not leave a minute too soon. While his family prepared for the journey west to Holland, only fifty miles south of Frankfurt German workers finished construction of the first of Hitler's concentration camps, venues of evil such as the world had never seen.

3 "The Kind of Child I'd Like to Have"

On August 16, 1933, Otto Frank officially registered with the Amsterdam Public Registration Office. After establishing the pectin business, Otto located what he thought would be an ideal home for his family at 37 Merwedeplein—an apartment on the second floor of a new string of buildings constructed in triangular shape around a small park.

The Franks Find a Home

Otto was pleased that because the new neighborhood appealed to families with young children, his daughters would find a ready supply of friends with whom to frolic in the trees and playing areas of the park. Edith and Margot joined Otto in December 1933, but the four-year-old Anne remained with her grandmother until the spring of 1934 when the apartment would be completely ready. While Otto was away at his office each workday, Edith and Margot arranged the furnishings in their new apartment. There was a tall nineteenth-century French secretary that had been handed to Edith by her parents, as well as a beautiful grandfather clock, a charcoal sketch of a large cat and two kittens, and other tasteful items.

When Anne arrived in Amsterdam, she quickly met a new friend, an event that would occur with regularity in her short life. One day a four-year-old girl named Hannah Elisabeth Pick-Goslar, whose family had also fled Germany in 1933, accompanied her mother's maid to the local store to purchase butter and milk. While there, they learned from other customers that another German family had moved in directly above them. Hannah met Anne that same day, and the two girls became fast friends. In her famous diary, Anne called Hannah "Lies Goosens."

Anne's Happy Childhood

Even at the tender age of four, Anne's lively interest in every event and her radiant face impressed people. Deep, dark-set eyes, with full eyebrows, peered out from above a warm smile. Short, black hair that fell barely to her ears topped a slender face and brittle frame. When Miep first met the little girl in Otto's office in 1933, she thought, "Now, here's the kind of child I'd like to have someday." Miep was enthralled that Anne's "dark, shining, alert large eyes, which dominated her delicate face, were drinking in everything around

Anne (at right) and Margot (center) enjoyed a relatively normal childhood despite the anti-Semitic fervor that was being stirred up in Europe during the 1930s.

her." Anne exhibited a "curiosity at things that for us adults were dull and commonplace: shipping boxes, wrapping paper, string, invoice holders."[19] One example of her budding intellect was that the youth readily mastered the language of her adopted nation.

When Miep walked Anne into her office, Anne "looked with fascination at my shiny black typewriter. I held her little fingers to the keys and pressed. Her eyes flashed when the keys jumped up and printed black letters onto the invoice rolled into the machine. Then I directed her attention to the window—just the kind of lively scene I thought any child would like. I was right. The view caught her interest: the streetcars, the bicycles, the passersby."[20]

After Anne started school, she and Hannah frequently spent Sundays together to do homework, or they traveled to the pectin company's office to play while Anne's father caught up on paperwork. Since each room at Otto's workplace contained its own telephone, Anne and Hannah loved to call each other and pretend they were shop owners. Occasionally, their more devilish sides emerged in childish pranks. Hannah remembered that at Anne's home, "we'd throw water out of the window onto the people walking by."[21]

The two families grew very close as the years passed. On Jewish holidays, the Franks often visited Hannah and her parents, while on other holidays, such as New Year's Eve, Hannah's family spent the night at the Frank home, where Anne and Hannah would sleep in the same room, then celebrate the new year with a jelly doughnut. Anne enjoyed blissful summer holidays in the company of her close friend and parents. During her years in

Anne (seated in front of her teacher in the back of the classroom) and her class at the Montessori School in Amsterdam. Anne had a rambunctious nature that won her many friends but also earned the disapproval of her instructors.

hiding, Anne pinned a photograph of Hannah to her bedroom wall to remind her of the good days.

In a book published long after the war, Hannah recalled that like most young people their age, Anne shared positive and negative qualities. "She was a stubborn girl. She was very good-looking. Everyone generally liked her, and she was always the center of attention at our parties. She was also the center of attention at school. She liked being important—that isn't a bad quality." Hannah added of her friend that "I remember that my mother, who liked her [Anne] very much, used to say, 'God knows everything, but Anne knows everything better.'"[22]

Fidgety and vibrant, Anne hated to be left alone with her thoughts. She preferred standing or sitting amidst a large crowd of friends, each one hopefully staring straight at her. Anne's constant chatter and even more frequent laughter ensured that she was one of the most popular girls in the neighborhood and at school. As Anne grew nearer her teenage years, she developed wide-ranging interests indicative of her restless nature. She loved attending movies and reading about movie stars. She adored going to parties or the local ice cream parlor, where she might catch the eye of a handsome boy. She enjoyed reading, Greek mythology, writing, animals, and spending the night at a friend's home.

Though Otto tried not to show favoritism between Margot and Anne, everyone noticed how he brightened a bit more in Anne's presence. Father and daughter seemed to share similar interests and outlooks, and Hannah claimed that Anne was "a bit spoiled, particularly by her father." While Edith and Margot evinced a quiet, religious side, Otto and Anne appeared more interested in people and events. However, Otto admitted after World War II that the impetuous Anne "was sometimes difficult" and he would have to administer "a quick spank" to get her attention.[23]

Anne at School

Anne started school in 1934 at Amsterdam's Sixth Public Montessori School. Margot accompanied her, as did Hannah, with whom Anne attended school until the Nazi takeover forced the Franks into hiding.

The popular Anne developed an army of friends and admirers, whose numbers seemed only to increase as the years passed. She and Hannah led what could be described as the "in" crowd in school, and many boys fixed their gazes on the attractive preteen, drawn by the silky black hair, which now reached to the shoulders, a slim frame, penetrating eyes, and all-encompassing smile. Anne did nothing to discourage the attention and even engaged in a bit of flirting. As Hannah explained of Anne, "I think she had more boys as friends than girls, especially when she was in the sixth grade and then in the first year at the Lyceum [all-Jewish school]. Boys really liked her. And she always liked it a lot when all the boys paid attention to her."

Consequently, Anne constantly fidgeted with her hair and brushed it to ensure she looked perfect. "Her hair kept her busy all the time," [24] stated Hannah later, who was also amused that Anne went to such extremes as purposely moving her shoulder out of its socket so that her classmates would have a good laugh.

Unfortunately, Anne's capers did not always sit well with her instructors, particularly her mathematics teacher. She talked so incessantly during class that the math teacher made her write an essay about "a chatterbox." Rather than bemoan her ill fortune, Anne wrote a paper in which she defended her actions as the result of heredity. She argued that since talking is a feminine trait, she should not be blamed for something over which she had no control.

The math teacher enjoyed the amusing explanation, but when Anne continued to disrupt class with her talking, he assigned a second paper titled, "Incurable Chatterbox." When this also failed to check Anne's behavior, he angrily admonished her in front of class and told her to write a paper on "Quack, quack, quack, says Mrs. Natterbeak." Anne escaped from

this seemingly impossible topic when her friend Sanne helped her write a poem about three baby ducklings who talked so much that the father swan bit them to death. In spite of these punishments, Anne continued to be a torment to her math teacher.

While Margot constantly brought home superb marks, Anne struggled along with mostly Bs, a few Cs, and an occasional D. She hated it when her parents held up Margot as an example of what she could be doing and became resentful of her sister because of this. However, Anne exhibited a talent for writing, and Hannah noticed that in the two years before Anne went into hiding, she constantly wrote in a diary.

Family Life

Otto Frank provided his family with a safe, comfortable living. Though not wealthy, the Franks never wanted for anything. While the family was proud of its Jewish heritage, Otto and Edith did not strictly follow their religion, preferring instead to teach their daughters to respect all faiths. Mr. Frank also explained, "Whether you are a Jew or a Christian, there is only one God. Only the paths to him are a little different." [25] The family even celebrated *Sinterklaas*, the December 5 feast of the Christian St. Nicholas, along with the rest of Holland, rather than observe only Jewish holidays such as Hanukkah.

The Franks spent much time together, frequently packing a few items and heading to the beach. Neither Otto nor Edith placed pressure on the girls to excel at school, because both parents believed that happiness was more important than good grades. While their daughters, especially Anne, enjoyed active social lives, Otto and Edith built a large group of friends with whom they spent time. Often, the Franks hosted gatherings in their apartment during which the adults discussed important issues of the day. Their guests included workers from Otto's business, such as Victor Kugler or Miep, who was not yet married to Jan Gies, and a neighboring dentist, Friedrich Pfeffer.

Otto's pectin business enjoyed a steady profit through the 1930s. A small staff included Miep, who handled the secretarial duties, and Kugler, Otto's top assistant, whom Miep described as "always serious, never joked." In 1938 Otto expanded the business to include herbs and spices used for making sausages. To manage the new department, he hired another Jewish refugee, Hermann van Pels, who fled Germany in 1937, to manage that portion. Mr.

Banning Books

Adolf Hitler knew that many books promoted democracy, espoused fair treatment of all people, and otherwise contradicted Nazi policies. In an attempt to protect the public from exposure to such "dangerous" ideas, he ordered mass book burnings. Susan D. Bachrach mentions what happened in her treatment, Tell Them We Remember: The Story of the Holocaust.

"During the spring of 1933, Nazi student organizations, professors, and librarians made up long lists of books they thought should not be read by Germans. Then, on the night of May 10, 1933, Nazis raided libraries and bookstores across Germany. They marched by torchlight in nighttime parades, sang chants, and threw books into huge bonfires. On that night more than 25,000 books were burned. Some were works of Jewish writers, including Albert Einstein and Sigmund Freud. Most of the books were by non-Jewish writers, including such famous Americans as Jack London, Ernest Hemingway, and Sinclair Lewis, whose ideas the Nazis viewed as different from their own and therefore not to be read."

Members of the Nazi police confiscate books in 1933. Hitler ordered the destruction of many texts that did not properly promote German ideals.

van Pels could name any spice after smelling it once and, according to Miep, was never "without a cigarette dangling from his mouth. He was a tall, large man, well-dressed, who stooped slightly when he walked."[26] By the beginning of the 1940s, eleven people worked at Opetka-Werke, including three or four traveling salesmen.

In January 1940, to make room for the increased volume of business, Otto moved his company to new offices in a four-story building along a canal at number 263 Prinsengracht. Miep and the other woman who did clerical work, Elly Voskuyl, shared a front office, while Kugler, van Pels, and Frank occupied offices to the rear.

Margot (at left), Anne (center), and their mother (at right) enjoy ice cream while on vacation. Though news of escalating violence toward Germany's Jews made the family wary, they felt secure in neighboring Holland.

The War Approaches

While Otto Frank built what he felt would be a safe life for his family in Amsterdam, events in Nazi Germany cast an ominous shadow across Europe. Firmly entrenched in power, Adolf Hitler immediately began to trample on the rights of anyone he considered an enemy—especially Jews. In September 1935 a series of anti-Jewish ordinances, the so-called Nuremberg laws, deprived Jews of many normal freedoms. Jews could no longer vote, marry non-Jews, or work in certain occupations. Hitler, who realized the threat posed to him by open discussion of ideas, also banned many books from public distribution in libraries and bookstores.

Hitler did not confine his actions to Germany. Desiring to regain land that was once part of Germany, in March 1936 he sent his troops to occupy the Rhineland, an area that had been under French control since the Treaty of Versailles. Two years later he proudly dispatched the German army into his homeland, Austria, to seal a takeover that had been negotiated through political channels. Otto, Miep, and the rest at the office listened with great trepidation to radio descriptions of this *anschluss* of Austria, for the German occupiers immediately clamped down on Austria's Jews.

Eva Edmunds, who was eight years old in 1936, recalled that in Austria, every Jew became a target for the German soldiers: "The streets were full of men in uniform, wearing armbands bearing the letters SA [*Sturmabteilung*] or SS [*Schutzstaffel*]. Many people were starting to wear the swastika on their coat lapels. These were the Aryans. Non-Aryans, I learned, were subjected to all kinds of indignities, like scrubbing the sidewalks, cleaning bathrooms, and the like."[27] Hearing of these developments from his office in neutral Holland, Otto Frank must have wondered whether Hitler would turn his possessive gaze west toward Amsterdam.

While the news from Austria worried the Franks, the shocking events of November

9–10 in Germany unnerved them more profoundly. Angered that a Jewish teenager had murdered a Nazi official in retaliation for the deportation of the boy's parents to Poland, mobs terrorized Jewish businesses, homes, and individuals throughout Germany. Over thirty thousand Jewish men disappeared into concentration camps, and numerous businesses were destroyed or had their windows shattered. Orchestrated by Hitler's officials, this destructive time became known as *Kristallnacht*, which means "night of the broken glass."

The message of that brutal night should have been clear. A former member of the Hitler Youth, an organization of young Germans who supported Hitler, later wrote that after *Kristallnacht* "no Jews could harbor any delusion that Hitler wanted Germany anything but *judenrein*, clean of Jews."[28] It appeared that Hitler's insane desire to eradicate the Jews was gaining momentum. Would the Franks be safe anywhere in Europe?

Is Amsterdam Safe?

Two of Edith Frank's brothers fled Germany at this time. Rather than remain in Europe, however, they settled in North America, where they felt sure they would be outside Hitler's grasp. Otto anguished over a similar move, but he believed that his family would be safe in the Netherlands, a nation that followed a strict policy of neutrality. With the Dutch government officially committed to the avoidance of involvement in any struggles among other European countries, there would be no reason, Otto concluded, for Hitler to invade his adopted homeland. By now his family had comfortably settled into Dutch life and Dutch schools, and his business was prospering. He was reluctant to pull up stakes and relocate to yet another foreign country.

Otto Frank counted on one other factor besides Dutch neutrality—the basic decency of German civilization. Unable to accept that an entire nation had gone mad, he contended that decent people would one day put an end to the hatred. He trusted that most Germans were good, and that the run of barbarism sponsored by the Nazis was only a brief nightmarish interlude.

Many Jews in Amsterdam disagreed with this hopeful outlook. Anne's friend Hannah, whose father believed that matters would greatly worsen before they improved, later stated that "Mr. Frank was an optimistic person. When he entered a room, the sun began to shine. He was always in a good mood." She concluded by comparing Mr. Frank to her father: "Ultimately, my father was right, but it was much more pleasant to hear what Mr. Frank had to say."[29]

In 1939 Edith's mother left Aachen to live with the Franks. Old Mrs. Hollander was so sickly that she had to remain in bed most of the time, but the Franks, especially Anne and Margot, loved having another family member among them. Before long, other people would be among them, but not family members. On September 1, 1939, Hitler unleashed his powerful armed forces in an unprecedented assault on Poland. World War II had begun.

Chapter

4 "Our World Was No Longer Ours"

The Franks watched military events with anxiety, for Hitler's vaunted German army swept aside opposing Polish forces as though they were minor nuisances. The Franks' slim hope was that Hitler would respect Dutch neutrality and refrain from invading the country. But even if Holland were spared, it appeared that Hitler would continue his announced policy of seizing land and would soon control much of Europe.

The Nazis Arrive

All doubt vanished on May 10, 1940, when Hitler unleashed his potent spring assault on western Europe. German paratroops, tanks, and soldiers overwhelmed meager Dutch resistance and poured into the Netherlands with terrifying speed and vigor.

Otto Frank and the other workers listened to the office radio for news of the momentous May 10 events. Miep stated that while everyone in the office was depressed and stunned, all life seemed to drain from Mr. Frank's face. The safety he thought he had found in neutral Holland had disappeared in moments. Rather than sheltering his loved ones from the Nazi beast, he had placed himself and his family in a very bad position—the certainty of life under Nazi rule.

Though the Dutch army resisted, they could do nothing to stop the German juggernaut. The queen, her family, and major government leaders were forced to flee to England; they left by night, on a ship. Miep wrote that "A wave of dejection went through us all" when they realized that no longer would their beloved Queen Wilhelmina or any of the political leaders be present.

The end arrived within four days. After German bombers had destroyed much of Rotterdam, one of the nation's major cities, military officials threatened to demolish Utrecht and Amsterdam as well unless the nation surrendered by May 14. One of Holland's top officers, General Winkelman, announced on radio that his forces would lay down their weapons on that day, and he asked that everyone remain calm and await further instructions.

"Now, suddenly, our world was no longer ours," recalled Miep. "Nothing worse could happen to us; we were no longer free." [30] In the days and years ahead, she would realize that much worse, indeed, could occur.

German soldiers advanced into Amsterdam on May 14. For the first time, Anne and Margot heard the sound of marching

The devastated Dutch city of Rotterdam. The small Dutch army could not stop Hitler's blitzkrieg, and the nation was forced to surrender in May 1940.

feet. They were trapped and at the mercy of the Nazi invaders.

Life Under Hitler's Rule

At first, conditions in Amsterdam continued as normal. Soldiers did not rush into neighborhoods and remove Jews; people were not shot in the streets; Anne and Margot attended the same school and played with the same friends. In fact, German soldiers who walked through the city were good-mannered and pleasant. "Often it seemed as though nothing had changed,"[31] Miep wrote of those days, but the relatively peaceful period would not last long.

Anti-Jewish comments started appearing in newspaper articles, and suddenly there was an entire series of laws, announced by Arthur Seyss-Inquart, the German high commissioner of the Netherlands: Jews were banned from theaters and restaurants, dismissed from key occupations, and subjected to other deprivations and indignities. In August Jewish refugees from Germany were required to register with German officials.

Books considered anti-German were removed from libraries and bookstores, fights broke out between Nazis and Jews, and signs appeared on park benches and in public places warning, "JEWS NOT WANTED HERE." "It started insidiously," reported Miep, "and as the long, dark winter settled over us, the noose around the Jewish neck began to tighten."[32]

To protect his business from the Nazis, in October Otto Frank switched legal control of the company to Victor Kugler and Jan Gies, Miep's fiancé, so that the company could be listed as Aryan-owned rather than Jewish-controlled. While he remained the actual director, his name no longer appeared as such on the official records.

The Jews Become Targets

The year 1941 opened ominously when the Nazis completed the first roundup of Jewish citizens. In February four hundred men and women were arrested and transported to Mauthausen concentration camp in Austria. Soon, relatives of those seized received word from Nazi authorities that these individuals, as Miep recalled, "had met with 'accidental' deaths. Families were notified of death by heart attack and tuberculosis. No one believed these stories of sudden accidental death."[33] Only two of these initial four hundred survived the war.

Attacks against Jews mounted. That same month a Dutch Nazi newspaper ran a story claiming that Jews with sharpened teeth had attacked a group of German soldiers, ripped open the victims' necks with their teeth, and drunk their blood.

Most Dutch citizens reacted with revulsion to German assaults on their nation's Jews. For three days in late February, the nation embarked on a general strike that shut down transportation and industry as a show of support for their Jewish cohorts. Though the action was uplifting to Jewish morale, the Nazis responded by arresting

A kiosk in Germany holds a banner that reads: "The Jews are our misfortune." Such propaganda permeated German media and subsequently infected the newspapers and airwaves of captured nations.

and beating many of the participants. To Hollanders like Miep and Kugler, who never hesitated to assist their fellow countrymen, the actions served as a stern reminder of what might happen to them.

Segregated Schools

One of the most shocking changes occurred when the school year resumed in 1941. Instead of continuing to attend the same school as their classmates, Anne and Margot had to switch to a Jewish educational institution, called the Lyceum, established by the Nazis to segregate the Jews into schools apart from other children. Though they would have the company of their Jewish friends, such as Hannah, Margot and Anne were now isolated from many of the boys and girls with whom they had grown up.

As in her first school, Anne experienced her share of problems with the nine teachers at the Lyceum, particularly Mr. Keesing, whom Anne called "the old fogey who teaches math."[34] One teacher, enraged by Anne's continual whispering with Hannah, grabbed Anne by the collar and put her in another room.

The most serious incident almost turned the entire class against the two friends. The French teacher spotted Hannah copying from Anne's paper during a test. He promptly gave both students a zero, but an upset Hannah blurted out to him that all the other members of the class had their books open under their desks. When the French teacher walked in the next day and handed out a new test to everyone, angry glares were directed toward Anne and Hannah.

Anne could not stand to be out of favor for long, so she penned an apology letter to her classmates. "Anne Frank and Hannah Pick-Goslar herewith offer the pupils of Class 16 II their sincere apologies for the cowardly betrayal. . . . It was an unpremeditated, thoughtless act, and we admit without hesitation that we are the only ones who should have been punished."[35] The heartfelt plea for forgiveness eased the other students' wrath and restored calm to the classroom.

Even in times of enormous stress, teenage girls notice teenage boys, and in this area Anne was far more advanced than the rest. Miep noticed that Anne's talk was now "spiced with chatter about particular young people of the opposite sex." Miep added reflectively:

It was as though the terrible events in the outside world were speeding up this little girl's development, as though Anne were suddenly in a hurry to know and experience everything. On the outside, Anne was a delicate, vivacious not-quite-twelve-year-old girl, but on the inside, a part of her was suddenly much older.[36]

Anne faced boys with the same supreme self-confidence with which she encountered any issue. While boasting that most of the boys had a crush on her, she claimed that she was an "expert" at handling her male classmates. For instance, many boys asked if they could ride home after school with her. Anne loved the attention, but if on the way home a boy asked Anne if he could speak to her father about dating her, "I swerve slightly on my bike, my schoolbag falls, and the young man feels obliged to get off his bike and hand me the bag, by which time I've

Dutch Resistance to Hitler

The Dutch resented Hitler's treatment of Jews and showed their opposition in numerous ways. In her book, The Holocaust, *Nora Levin mentions what the Dutch did when Jews were forced to wear yellow stars or when other anti-Jewish laws were enacted.*

"The Nazi decrees against the Dutch Jews aroused deep resentment among the Dutch and opposition to them became a badge of patriotism. Not only had their workers led the bold strikes of February 1941, but students went on strike to protest the dismissal of Jewish teachers. To express their sympathy with the wearers of yellow stars, many Dutch citizens wore yellow flowers on their coat lapels. In Rotterdam, signs were plastered on walls throughout the city reminding the Dutch to show respect to Jews on the streets. Non-Jews often shopped for their Jewish neighbors. Intellectuals were outspoken. Both the Protestant and Catholic churches urged resistance to the anti-Jewish decrees."

Otto Frank (wearing hat) and Anne (to his left) with other guests attending Miep and Jan Gies's wedding in 1941. Although German authorities had begun discriminatory measures against Holland's Jews, the Franks and other families tried to live fairly normal lives.

switched the conversation to another topic."[37] Should any young man take matters too far and attempt to hold her arm or blow a kiss at her, she acted insulted and asked him to immediately leave.

Like many youth her age, Anne formed speedy judgments of her classmates. She labeled one girl "a detestable, sneaky, stuck-up, two-faced gossip who thinks she's grown up," and stated that while she had a crush on a boy named Sallie Springer, she preferred to avoid him because "rumor has it that he's gone all the way."[38]

Besides dating and wondering who liked whom, Anne fretted about her grades. She wrote near the end of one school year that "The entire class is quaking in its boots" because the teachers were about to decide which students to promote. "If you ask me," Anne wrote, "there are so many dummies that about a quarter of the class should be kept back, but teachers are the most unpredictable creatures on earth."[39]

Anne was promoted, though she hardly gained praise with her mixture of Bs, Cs, and one D. She stated that her parents did not "worry about report cards,

good or bad. As long as I'm healthy and happy and don't talk back too much, they're satisfied." When Margot's grades earned her a promotion with honors, however, Anne concluded sarcastically, "Brilliant, as usual."[40] It is impossible to tell, today, whether the remark about Margot indicated that Anne felt her parents compared her to her older sister or that Anne's intensely competitive nature made it difficult for her to accept Margot's accomplishments.

The Nazi Terror Intensifies

Anne soon would long for the days when boys and grades were her major worries. It seemed that every day the Nazis came for more Jewish men, women, and children. Otto Frank became so alarmed at the increasing persecution that in January 1942, shortly after the death of his mother-in-law, he attempted to obtain a permit to leave the country. His alarm had come too late, however; the exit visa was denied.

Nazi laws required every Jew to wear a Star of David. Marked Jews became easy targets for anti-Semitic hate speech and violence.

Trapped in a nation that once had appeared to be the family's refuge, Otto started to make plans to go into hiding. After deciding to use the back rooms at his business, Otto quietly informed Miep and Jan Gies, Victor Kugler, and Bep Voskuijl, who quickly offered their help.

Gradually, like a spreading blanket that slowly suffocated the lives of those covered by it, anti-Jewish laws stripped the Franks of everything they had considered normal. In the spring of 1942 the Nazi occupation government ordered Jews to have a yellow, six-pointed star the size of a baseball sewn onto each item of clothing. Bearing the Dutch word for Jew—*Jood*—in the middle, the stars simplified identification of Jews on the streets for Nazi police. The Franks chafed at the humiliation of having to wear the stars, which marked Jews as an undesirable group, but they had no choice. One Jewish woman recalled that, "Wearing the yellow star, with which we were branded . . . as if we were criminals, was a form of torture. Every day when I went out in the street I had to struggle to maintain my composure."[41]

Workers at Otto Frank's office tried to ignore the star when their employer first wore it, but they knew that the embarrassment of the situation tore at his insides.

Miep labeled the next anti-Jewish measure, which required every Jew to hand in his bicycle, in perfect condition, by June 1942, "the lowest trick of all."[42] Since bicycles provided the main means of transportation for most Dutch citizens, including Otto, Anne, and Margot, a resident without a bicycle found his or her mobility drastically limited.

Another new law prevented Jews from using streetcars or any other method of public transportation. Thus, without a bicycle, Otto Frank had to walk to work each morning. Miep watched him as he shuffled into the office, already exhausted before the work day had commenced:

> Although Mr. Frank gave the impression of everything's being normal, I could see that he was worn out. Now, because he was not allowed on the streetcar, he had to walk many miles to the office each day, and then return home on foot at night. It was impossible for me to imagine the strain that he, Mrs. Frank, Margot, and Anne were under. Their situation was never discussed, and I did not ask.[43]

Anne, who twelve days earlier had received the diary that was to immortalize her, frequently mentioned the oppressive conditions. On June 24 she complained that the heat was "sweltering. Everyone is huffing and puffing, and in this heat I have to walk everywhere. Only now do I realize how pleasant a streetcar is, but we Jews are no longer allowed to make use of this luxury; our own two feet are good enough for us."[44]

In another diary entry, Anne listed some of the anti-Jewish laws she had to obey: Jews could shop in stores only between 3:00 P.M. and 5:00 P.M.; they could use only Jewish-owned barbershops and beauty parlors; they had to remain in their homes from 8:00 P.M. until 6:00 A.M.; they could not go to movies or theatrical performances; they could not use tennis courts or athletic fields; and they could not visit Christian friends in their homes. "Some of the anti-Jewish orders were laughable," [45] Miep stated, citing the ordinances forbidding Jews from keeping pigeons and from using public swimming pools.

The onerous new laws burdened all Jews, but they were particularly harsh for teenagers, whose expanding interest in the world about them crashed headlong against the Nazi restraints. Just when kids began to notice the opposite sex and wanted to attend movies and parties, they had to forego such normal activities because of the anti-Jewish laws.

Miep noticed that while Mr. and Mrs. Frank and Margot shared little of their feelings about these rules, Anne "spoke candidly about all kinds of things. She was aware of everything going on in the outside world. She was very indignant about the injustices being heaped on the Jewish people." [46]

Anne Receives Her Diary

On June 12, 1942, an excited Anne woke at 6:00 A.M., eager to rush out of her room to begin her thirteenth birthday. Since she was not permitted up until 6:45, she impatiently counted the minutes, then

Segregated Schools

One of the harshest anti-Semitic steps taken by the Nazis was forcing Jewish children into separate schools. One woman, Fritzie Fritzshall, recalls what that day was like for her as a little girl, in an interview she granted to the United States Holocaust Memorial Museum.

"The night before going to school, my friend who was not Jewish—she and I slept in our home. Slept in the same bed, played as children do. I remember my mother opening the door and telling us to go to sleep, because we were being noisy and the next day was school. She and I got up in the morning to go to school, one morning. When we came to school, she was allowed to walk in and the door was closed to me. I was told I was not allowed to walk into class anymore. I needed to go home, because I was Jewish. . . . I remember going home and crying, and not understanding why I was not allowed to go to school anymore. A few minutes later, my two brothers came home crying. They too were sent back home, and were told not to go to school anymore."

exploded from bed and hurried into the living room to open her presents. While she received a bounty of gifts, including a bouquet of roses, a blouse, a game, some money, and a gift certificate for two books, her most cherished prize was the gift handed to her by her father—a diary. She later wrote that "*you* (italics hers) were the first thing I saw."[47]

After the early celebration, Anne walked to school with a friend, where she handed out cookies during recess. Since it was her birthday, the gym teacher allowed Anne to select which game the class would play. She chose soccer, following which everyone gathered around and sang "Happy Birthday."

Though delighted to finally own a diary in which to record her thoughts, Anne at first doubted that the red-orange, check-

The diary Anne received on her birthday in 1942. Its contents would survive the war and bear witness to the horrors of the Holocaust.

ered volume of blank pages would have any significance beyond what it was—a place to scribble hopes, fears, and dreams. She worried that keeping a diary might even be futile, since "it seems to me that later on neither I nor anyone else will be interested in the musings of a thirteen-year-old schoolgirl." However, this fleeting thought quickly disappeared. "Oh well, it doesn't matter. I feel like writing, and I have an even greater need to get all kinds of things off my chest."[48]

Anne felt this need because, while she was popular and knew everybody, she felt the lack of a silent, never critical friend with whom she might share her deepest secrets. As she confided to her diary only eight days after receiving it, "I have a throng of admirers who can't keep their adoring eyes off me," but she wanted "the diary to be my friend, and I'm going to call this friend *Kitty*."[49]

A New Boyfriend

Three days after this entry, Anne had something special to record—a new boyfriend, sixteen-year-old Hello Silberberg. Each day he met Anne and escorted her to the Lyceum. Shortly after the young Jewish couple had begun this innocent arrangement, Anne introduced Hello to her parents. The two then left for a long walk about town during which they forgot about the time. With Nazi soldiers and the Green Police on the prowl, a Jew outside after the 8:00 P.M. curfew placed his or her life in jeopardy, so when Hello and Anne finally appeared at 8:10, a distraught Otto Frank made Anne promise to be home by 7:50 P.M. from then on.

A photo of Anne in 1940. Her life would change dramatically over the next few years.

7:50 P.M. from then on.

Anne confided to her diary on July 1, only five days before the family had to flee into hiding, that "In everything he says or does, I can see that Hello is in love with me." She wrote that while her mother and Margot liked Hello, she herself was preoccupied by a crush on another boy, Peter Schiff. "I love Peter as I've never loved any-

one,"[50] concluded the youthful diarist.

Her exhilarating thoughts about boys and love, so typical of a teenage girl, came to a sudden halt during an early July stroll through the neighborhood with her father. Otto explained that because conditions were so rapidly deteriorating for Jews in Amsterdam, the family would have to go into hiding. Anne asked him why he mentioned such a depressing notion, and her father added that he had been storing many of their possessions with other people. "We don't want our belongings to be seized by the Germans. Nor do we want to fall into their clutches ourselves. So we'll leave of our own accord and not wait to be hauled away."

Noticing that his words frightened Anne, Otto quickly added, "Don't you worry. We'll take care of everything. Just enjoy your carefree life while you can." Shortly afterward, Anne wrote in her diary for July 5: "Oh, may these somber words not come true for as long as possible."[51]

Anne had only hours left to enjoy her carefree life, for the next day the family moved to the Secret Annex. She had no time even to say goodbye to anyone, for Otto Frank had worked out an elaborate scheme to trick neighbors into believing the family had fled to Switzerland.

For the indeterminate future, a normal teenage existence was denied Anne. The adult world, with its hatred and wars, had stretched a destructive hand into Anne's

5 "A Thief Was Safe and a Jew Was Not"

A few days after the Franks had gone into hiding, Hannah rode over to her friend's house. Though she rang the doorbell for a long time, no one answered. Perplexed, Hannah was about to leave when the Franks' tenant, Mr. Goldschmidt, opened the door.

"What do you want? What have you come for?" asked Mr. Goldschmidt.

When Hannah explained the purpose for her visit, the tenant replied, "Don't you know that the entire Frank family has gone to Switzerland?" [52]

Stunned that her close friend had so quickly fled the country, Hannah returned home to tell her mother.

The Franks Settle In

Cut off from the rest of Dutch society, the Franks transformed the Secret Annex into something they could call home. All during their first day the four unloaded boxes, cleaned rooms, and hung materials on walls. Though forced to share a bedroom with Margot, Anne added her personality to the room by pasting to the walls photographs of movie stars such as Greta Garbo, Ginger Rogers, and Ray Milland.

Later in the afternoon Miep arrived for her first of what would become daily visits to her friends in the Annex. She noticed that while Otto and Anne scurried busily about, "Mrs. Frank and Margot were like lost people, drained of blood, in conditions of complete lethargy." [53]

On the other hand Anne and her father appeared unconcerned about their new surroundings. Miep spotted a change in Mr. Frank. Whereas he used to act somewhat nervous, "he now displayed a veneer of total control; a feeling of safety and calm emanated from him. I could see that he was setting a calm example for the others." [54] His pretense apparently worked with Anne, who wrote in her diary that while she would never feel at home in the Annex, "that doesn't mean I hate it. It's more like being on vacation in some strange [hotel]." The Franks worked all day "until we fell exhausted into our clean beds at night," [55] then repeated the process during the next two days.

Eager to learn whether his plan to make people think they had escaped had worked, Mr. Frank asked Miep and Jan to visit their apartment. "The Franks have vanished," Mr. Goldschmidt told them, and he handed them a slip of paper he had found which contained an address in Maastricht, a Dutch city along a possible escape route to Switzerland. "Mr. Frank has family in Switzerland," Goldschmidt

A visitor to the museum at the Anne Frank House looks at Anne's wall of movie star photos and family snapshots.

volunteered. "Perhaps they've fled to Switzerland?"[56] He then shared neighborhood rumors that the Franks had driven away one night in a large car, that they had fled on bicycles, or even that the Nazis had barged in and taken them away. Otto Frank's plan had succeeded.

By slow degrees, events chipped away at Anne's initial thought that life in hiding would resemble a vacation. When Miep returned from her visit to the apartment, Anne bombarded her with questions, particularly about her pet. "What about Moortje? Have you seen my cat, Moortje?"[57] Miep could tell her nothing, since asking Mr. Goldschmidt any questions might have aroused suspicion. Anne wrote only a few days after leaving her cat that Moortje was "my weak spot. I miss her every minute of the day, and no one knows how often I think of her; whenever I do, my eyes fill with tears."[58]

The most terrifying specter, however, was the thought of being captured. On the first Friday evening in the Annex, the family sneaked downstairs after the work-

ers had departed to listen to a radio broadcast from the British Broadcasting Corporation (BBC). Each night the BBC sent out news reports and information to listeners in Nazi-occupied Europe, but Anne was so afraid they would be discovered that she begged her father to take her back upstairs.

"Whatever we do, we're very afraid the neighbors might hear or see us," she told her diary. "I'm terrified our hiding place will be discovered and that we'll be shot."[59] Anne had found comfort behind the safety of the Annex's walls, which had become the last barrier holding at bay those who hunted for her.

The Van Pels Family Arrives

On July 13 three other people joined the Franks in the Secret Annex—Otto's business partner, Hermann van Pels, Hermann's wife, Auguste, and their sixteen-year-old son, Peter. Anne's first impressions of the teenager

A photo of the rear of the building that housed the Secret Annex. The Franks and their friends would remain confined in the Annex for two years.

were unfavorable. Peter—tall, dark-haired, quiet—was "a shy, awkward boy whose company won't amount to much,"[60] she scribbled in her diary. Anne had little to say about Mr. van Pels, a balding man in his forties, or Mrs. van Pels, a dark-haired woman who appeared to be more accustomed to ease and comfort than to privations.

However, the two families quickly settled into a routine in their new accommodations. Constructed in 1635, the building housing the Secret Annex could be entered from three separate doors that faced the canal. A door on the right led directly to a warehouse on the building's ground floor, where three workers ground, weighed, and packed spices. Only one laborer—Bep Voskuijl's father—knew that the Franks had moved into the Annex. A door to the left took a visitor to storage areas on the third and fourth floors. These doors were not used by anyone in the Annex nor by their helpers in the offices.

Upon stepping through the middle door, a visitor would walk to the main office, where Miep and Bep greeted customers and worked at their desks. A hallway opened to a second office, which van Pels and Victor Kugler shared. From this office, a small corridor led to a landing containing the entrance to the Secret Annex resting in the rear of the building.

Upon passing through the entrance, a person could either turn to the right and enter the Franks' living area, or move straight ahead to the steps that ascended to the fourth floor, which the van Pelses occupied. The Franks had two bedrooms—a larger one used by the parents and a smaller one for the girls. The washing room with toilet, which all seven shared, was on the Franks' floor. Directly overhead lay the van Pelses' quarters—a huge family room that also served as a kitchen/dining area and as a bedroom for Mr. and Mrs. van Pels, and Peter's room. A ladder stretched from Peter's room to an attic, which was used to store food.

Daily Routine

Each morning an alarm clock awakened the occupants at 6:45 so that they would have enough time to get ready for the day ahead before the workers arrived in the warehouse below. Once the laborers appeared, everyone had to remain perfectly quiet until the lunch break.

Under the guidance of Otto Frank, Anne, Margot, and Peter used the time to study languages, algebra, geometry, geography, and history. While Anne despised doing "that wretched math every day," she loved reading and peppered her diary with comments about books. She especially enjoyed the author Cissy van Marxveldt and stated, with obvious optimism, that she would one day emerge from her ordeal, that "I'm definitely going to let my own children read her books too."[61] Each week Miep brought in books from a local bookstore owned by a close friend.

Around 12:45, when the workers left for lunch, the group could move around and gather for their own lunch break. Frequently joined by Miep or one of the other helpers from below, they listened to radio reports from the BBC. By 1:45, when the afternoon shift began, everyone had to resume total silence. At 5:30, Bep or Miep would affirm that all the workers had gone home, and the seven could freely move about, making all the noise they desired.

Anne most looked forward to the daily visits from Miep and her husband, Jan. As Miep recalled, the men would collect around Jan for news while the women flocked to Miep, "Except for always-curious Anne. Anne was always at the forefront of all the discussions, men's and women's."[62] Miep could hardly step into the Annex before Anne rushed forward and "greeted all of us visitors with a barrage of questions and inquiries."

The evenings were more relaxing, since the family did not have to worry

War's End in 1943?

Amidst the daily chaos, each member in the Annex as well as their helpers kept alive the dream that the war would soon end. In her book about those days, Anne Frank Remembered, *Miep recalls one such occurrence.*

"We were all sure that the war would be over in 1943. . . .

Jan and I, all of us, followed the battle of Stalingrad. None of us had ever heard reports of such a bitter and bloody battle before. Inch by inch, the Germans were being beaten and left to freeze in the frozen snow. Good, I thought; let them all freeze, and Hitler as well.

The word 'surrender' was being used for the first time over the BBC. The Germans were on the verge of surrender. We dared to hope, but no one could ever imagine the word 'surrender' coming out of Hitler's mouth.

But surrender they did, on February 2. The following day, we gathered around the radios, tingling from head to toe with the news and squeezing each other's hands. . . .What glee we felt! We hoped it was the beginning of the end."

about workers hearing them. Blackout curtains blanketed each window, however, so that no lights could be seen from outside. Often, Anne and Margot completed paperwork in the office that had been left for them by Miep and Bep or walked about the downstairs offices. Others in the group, lacking a normal bathtub, cleaned themselves as best they could in the lavatory washtub. By 9:00 P.M. activities ceased and both families prepared for bed: Margot set up her folding cot, Mr. and Mrs. van Pels shuffled chairs and tables to make room for their bed, and Anne retreated to her five-foot divan, to which she added a few chairs for extra length. Before 10:00 P.M. everyone had settled in.

Various arrangements were made to ensure a steady, if not varied, supply of food. To obtain most items, a person needed to have a government-issued ration card, which gave permission to purchase the stipulated item. Early on, therefore, Miep's husband had gathered the seven ration cards from the members of the Annex and exchanged them for new ones forged by a secret Dutch organization working against the Nazis. This enabled Miep to walk into a store and purchase food with the fake ration cards. Since wartime cuts off many sources of supplies, Miep had to make the best of what she could find.

Compared to other Jewish families, the Franks and the van Pelses lived comfort-

Visitors to the Anne Frank House view a model of the Secret Annex.

ably in those first weeks in the Annex. They had a safe, warm place in which to stay, and most importantly, they were together as families. However, hovering over them was the frightful notion that at any moment the Nazis might locate their secure world. They could never let their guard down until war's end—whenever that might come.

As an extra precaution, Otto Frank asked Bep's father to make a bookcase that could be placed in front of the entrance to the Secret Annex. Fastened with hinges, the bookcase could be swung open to allow entry. Closed tightly, the bookcase provided an excellent cover.

Miep knew that her friends "were in a prison, a prison with locks inside the doors," and made sure that whenever she visited them, she "put on an air of calm and good cheer that it was otherwise impossible to feel anywhere in Amsterdam anymore." She loved visiting with Anne and answering her ever-lengthy list of questions, and she marveled that of the many gifts given to this young girl, Anne thought her best feature was her thick, shining black hair: "She liked to comb it several times a day to keep it healthy and to bring out its sheen. . . . She set her hair nightly in pin curls to turn up the ends."[63]

Miep quickly formed judgments of the other members. Margot and Peter "were quite withdrawn, always part of the background." While she found Mrs. Frank to be "kind and orderly, very quiet but aware of everything that went on around her," Miep regarded Mrs. van Pels as "temperamental, flirty, chatty." She enjoyed Mr. van Pels's stream of jokes but found him to be "something of a pessimist, always smoking, and somewhat restless." Her favorite was Otto Frank, whom she labeled "the most

logical, the one who balanced everyone out. He was the leader, the one in charge. When a decision had to be made, all eyes turned to Mr. Frank."[64]

Period of Adjustment

From the beginning everyone in the Annex knew that Anne recorded thoughts and conversations in her diary, which she kept in Otto's briefcase. Everyone also knew that many of the entries could have implicated Miep, Kugler, and the other helpers if the diary had fallen into Nazi hands. Fortunately for future generations, however, no one stopped Anne from indulging in this very risky form of expression.

During the early months of confinement, the diary held mainly the normal musings of a teenage girl. Typical entries referred to clashes between the writer and her parents, particularly her mother, whom Anne said "treats me like a baby, which I can't stand." She complained about her mother's "dreadful sermons" and observed that the two took "the opposite view of everything." She resented being told to be like Margot, whom Anne claimed was "too weak-willed and passive to suit me; she lets herself be swayed by others and always backs down under pressure. I want to have more spunk!" Anne hated "the nasty words, mocking looks and accusations that she [her mother] hurls at me day after day, piercing me like arrows from a tightly strung bow, which are nearly impossible to pull from my body." However, almost in the same breath she mentioned feeling guilty. "I hope Mother will *never* (italics Anne's) read this or anything else I've written."[65]

Fights with Mother

In her October 3, 1942, diary entry, a frustrated Anne explodes about her feelings toward her mother.

"Yesterday Mother and I had another run-in and she really kicked up a fuss. She told Daddy all my sins and started to cry, which made me cry too, and I already had such an awful headache. I finally told Daddy that I love 'him' more than I do Mother, to which he replied that it was just a passing phase, but I don't think so. I simply can't stand Mother, and I have to force myself not to snap at her all the time, and to stay calm, when I'd rather slap her across the face."

Consequently, Anne felt much closer to her father, whom she affectionately called Pim: "Daddy's a sweetheart," she wrote, who "usually comes to my defense. Without him I wouldn't be able to stick it out here."[66] Anne and Otto shared many thoughts, and whenever he could he reminded Anne that her mother loved her and advised her to try to be more understanding.

The early months inside the Annex proved awkward, as the two families attempted to peacefully exist in such close quarters. While they enjoyed lighter moments, especially around the dinner table, where Mr. van Pels loved to regale everyone with a steady stream of jokes, friction arose. The Franks were astonished at the adult van Pelses' selfishness. Each time Miep or Jan entered, Mr. van Pels asked for cigarettes, and because Mrs. van Pels did all the cooking, her husband received the best food. "The choicest potatoes, the tastiest morsel, the tenderest bit of whatever there is, that's Madame's motto. 'The others can all have

their turn, as long as I get the best,'"[67] complained Anne to her diary.

Anne was also astonished that the van Pelses argued with each other in front of the rest. In September she mentioned that the couple had had "a terrible fight. I've never seen anything like it, since Mother and Father wouldn't dream of shouting at each other like that." Since Mr. van Pels was resentful whenever anyone disagreed with his opinions, sooner or later the strong-willed Anne was certain to butt heads with him. As early as August she wrote that "Mr. [van Pels] and I are always at loggerheads with each other."[68]

Though unable to move about in the outside world, the seven received a steady flow of reports from their helpers and from the news broadcast on the BBC. They gathered around the radio in hopes of catching any information about the progress of the Allied armies—the forces led by the United States, England, and Soviet Union—in their battles against Hitler. They prayed that one day the Allied armies would pour into the Netherlands, defeat

Hitler's forces, and set them free. All they could do was sit and wait—and hope that no one discovered their hiding place.

Constant scares instilled panic and disrupted their peace. Near the end of October one incident so frightened Anne that her hands shook for two hours afterward. Unable to open the bookcase because one of the hooks that fastened it had stuck, Miep failed to alert the occupants of the Annex that a worker would be in the office to fill the fire extinguishers during the lunch break. When a sudden pounding took place near the bookcase, Anne and everyone else froze in terror. "We all turned white with fear," wrote Anne, who added

that "I was so scared I nearly fainted at the thought of this total stranger managing to discover our wonderful hiding place."[69] Anne had imagined one of Hitler's soldiers trying to beat down the door.

Consequently, in this month the first mention of a concentration camp appeared in Anne's diary. Upon learning that many Dutch Jews had been arrested and taken to a dismal camp in Holland called Westerbork, she asked herself a disturbing question: If it was that bad in a concentration camp in Holland, how much worse must it be for those sent to "faraway and uncivilized places where the Germans are sending them? We assume that most of them are being murdered. The English radio says they're being gassed. Perhaps that's the quickest way to die."[70]

Most of the time Anne, Margot, and Peter pushed aside these thoughts and focused on their schoolwork or dreamed of better days. References to boys, parties, and outside activities dotted Anne's diary, though she barely gave Peter a second thought. "He's an obnoxious boy who lies around on his bed all day, only rousing himself to do a little carpentry work before returning to his nap. What a dope!"[71]

Friedrich Pfeffer Arrives

Anne's attitudes and opinions, and the topics of her diary, would shortly change. In November 1942 the families learned that an eighth person was joining them in hiding—Friedrich Pfeffer, a Jewish dentist whom the Franks had known since their earliest days in Amsterdam. Known as Albert Dussel in Anne's diary, the dentist could hardly believe that the Franks were still in the country because he, like others

---

Rumors About Westerbork

Gradually, the terrors swirling about on the outside began to permeate Anne's diary. Before 1942 ended, she had already written of the unspeakable, as in this entry from October 9.

"Our many Jewish friends and acquaintances are being taken away in droves. The Gestapo [Nazi secret police] is treating them very roughly and transporting them in cattle cars to Westerbork, the big camp in Drenthe [a northeastern province of Holland] to which they're sending all the Jews. Miep told us about someone who'd managed to escape from there. It must be terrible in Westerbork. The people get almost nothing to eat, much less to drink, as water is available only one hour a day, and there's only one toilet and sink for several thousand people. Men and women sleep in the same room, and women and children often have their heads shaved."

Allied planes bombed factories and military installations in Germany and German-occupied territories. To the Franks, the sound of explosions signaled the advance of Allied armies, yet the family also feared the bombers might accidentally destroy the Annex.

on the outside, had believed the story about the family's flight to Switzerland.

During the winter of 1942–1943 Miep noticed "a flagging of energy up in the Annex." The cheerfulness and relief at being sheltered had been replaced by a subdued manner, "as though some of the spirit had gone out of the people upstairs."[72] To help, she and Bep handed each person little gifts and poems on St. Nicholas Day. This kindness, along with a joyful Hanukkah celebration and a feast of sausages, restored some of the vitality.

So, too, did further news from the war. In slow stages, the Allied armies advanced across northern Africa, crossed the Mediterranean Sea to the island of Sicily, then battled their way onto the European mainland near Rome. Each Allied victory meant that the people in the Annex were one step closer to deliverance.

"We jumped for joy," Anne reported, writing that she finally saw "Hope for an end to the war, hope for peace." When Mr. van Pels warned in early May that the conflict would not cease until the end of 1943 Anne wrote "That's a very long time, and yet it's possible to hold out until then."[73]

Another comforting event was the sound of Allied bombers as they flew toward their targets in the Netherlands or Germany. Like friends passing by in the daylight or at night, the aircraft provided solace to a group sorely in need of reasons to hope for the future. Yet no matter how uplifting the presence of the friendly aircraft was, it created moments of sheer terror for those in the Annex, who at any moment might have been hit by an errant bomb, by falling antiaircraft shells, or by damaged bombers plummeting out of control. One night a bomber crashed only blocks from the Annex and ignited a series of explosions and fires. Since the group could not leave the Annex for the safety of a bomb shelter, they nightly ran the risk of dying in their hiding place.

Miep wrote that the people "lived constantly with the feeling that they were about to be bombed, or burned, or crashed upon."[74] Ironically, something that was designed to shorten the war also added to Anne's terrors. On March 10, 1943, she wrote, "I still haven't gotten over my fear of planes and shooting [antiaircraft fire], and I crawl into Father's bed nearly every night for comfort. I know it sounds childish, but wait until it happens to you!"[75]

Break-ins and Food Shortages

As the war dragged on, food shortages plagued the Netherlands. Break-ins of warehouses and shops rocketed as people whose livelihoods had been destroyed by the war scavenged for sustenance. Otto's business was burglarized several times, and these events petrified the Annex group be- cause they could never be sure whether the noises made by thieves were caused by hungry Dutchmen or by German soldiers coming to arrest them. Afterward they wondered for days whether the burglars had noticed anything suspicious that they might report to authorities in hopes of receiving a reward. As Miep mentioned, "The times were such that a thief was safe and a Jew was not."[76]

As a result, from time to time tempers flared in the Annex and people were afraid to say much at dinner because someone might take it in the wrong manner. A distraught Anne stated that "A good hearty laugh would help," but added frustratedly, "we've almost forgotten how to laugh."

Laughs would occur far less frequently after September 1943, for everyone worried about a warehouse worker named van Maaren: "[He] is getting suspicious about the Annex,"[77] Anne wrote. Did he know of the existence of the hiding place? If so, would he turn its occupants in before the Allies arrived to free them?

Chapter

6 Crushed Dreams and Cherished Hopes

Concern that someone on the outside might discover their hiding place was one thing; worry about a worker inside the warehouse was even more serious. Van Maaren walked into the building five days a week and, if he looked around with a wary eye, he was bound to detect something unusual eventually. Van Maaren knew that at one time there had been an entrance to some back rooms, and more than once he had spotted Miep or Bep carrying bags of groceries into the office.

Love Blooms

In spite of the situation, normal teenage interests coexisted with danger in an unstable alliance. On January 6, 1944, Anne first recorded that she had developed a huge crush on the only boy available—Peter. She referred to his "dark blue eyes" and claimed that "I saw his shyness, and I melted." [78]

The next month she climbed into the attic to retrieve some potatoes and, when she passed through Peter's room "he gave me such a warm, tender look that I started glowing inside." When she later returned to his room, Peter talked about his plans after the war and how he frequently felt so worthless. Anne's constricted world sud-

denly broadened, and she hoped that "something beautiful is going to develop between Peter and me, a kind of friendship and a feeling of trust." [79]

By the end of March Anne and Peter had spent so much time together that Anne's mother started to worry. Anne shrugged off the concern and continued heading into Peter's room.

Despite the time they spent together, the shy Peter kept his distance. The brasher Anne wanted "so much for him to kiss me, but that kiss is taking its own sweet time." She warned herself to be patient, and on April 15, which she called "a red-letter day for me," her wish came true. As they sat together that night, Peter suddenly pulled Anne closer to him, caressed her arms and played with her hair, and then kissed her, "half on my left cheek and half on my ear." When he kissed her on the lips twelve days later, an ecstatic Anne could hardly contain her joy. "What could be nicer than sitting before an open window, enjoying nature, listening to the birds sing, feeling the sun on your cheeks and holding a darling boy in your arms?" [80] For the first time since she had disappeared into hiding, Anne felt like a normal teenager.

About the same time Anne's dreams for her future solidified. On March 29, 1944, she learned from a radio broadcast that after

Anne writes at her desk in 1940. One of Anne's ambitions was to be a journalist. Although she did not fulfill that dream, Anne's diary exemplifies her writing talent.

the war, the Dutch government intended to collect diaries and letters written during the conflict. Thinking that hers might be among those published, she started to edit the diary to make it more presentable. While still writing daily entries, Anne added thoughts and improved the grammar of her comments of 1942 to 1943.

This project renewed her determination to succeed as a writer. She mentioned her eagerness "to get on with life, to become a journalist, because that's what I want!" She was driven to this goal because she wanted to achieve something of note. "I can't imagine having to live like Mother, Mrs. [van Pels] and all the women who go about their work and are then forgotten. I need to have something besides a husband and children to devote myself to! I don't want to have lived in vain like most people." She added that "I want to go on living even after my death!"[81] She planned to submit an article to a magazine under an assumed name, and after the war she hoped to publish a book based on her experiences in hiding called *The Secret Annex*.

This endeavor allowed Anne to reevaluate her earlier writings and compare her current ideas and attitudes to those she held when she first went into hiding. She was amazed at her "childish innocence" in 1942 but concluded she had noticeably matured during the interval. She thought that the Anne Frank who entered the Annex was "a pleasant, amusing, but superficial girl, who has nothing to do with me." She admitted that in arguments with her mother she saw "things only from my own perspective" and concluded that while her mother did not understand her, "I didn't understand her either."[82]

Another sign of her maturity was that she started to write about the physical changes occurring in her body. In late October 1942 she confided to her diary that "I long to get my period—then I'll really be grown up." By early 1944, after menstruating three times, she happily stated that "what's happening to me is so wonderful."[83] She called the events "a sweet secret" and looked forward to each one.

Problems in the Annex

Because of their confinement, the members in the Annex experienced problems in areas that normally are handled in rou-

tine fashion. A five-inch growth spurt by Anne made all the clothes she had brought with her too small. Margot was growing, too, and Miep noticed that inadequate shoes pinched at the teens' feet, and their threadbare clothes offered a pathetic sight, especially Anne's, "who was turning into not-so-little Anne before our very eyes. She was simply bursting out of her clothes, and her body was changing shape as well."[84] Margot had to wear a bra that was two sizes too small.

Because Anne had not had proper light for reading, her eyesight deteriorated. In 1943 Miep offered to take her outside to an eye doctor she trusted, but the thought of leaving the safe haven proved too frightening to Anne, who "went white around the mouth with fear."[85] Otto decided not to risk such a venture, so Anne spent the rest of her life with poor eyesight and headaches.

As the days passed, obtaining sufficient food for the eight became more difficult. By the spring of 1943 Miep encountered long lines outside of stores, only to eventually bring home "a few beans, some wilted lettuce, half-rotted potatoes—food that when I got it home was bad and made us sick."[86] To make the food more bearable, Anne pretended that it was delicious and, without looking at it, stuffed it quickly into her mouth and swallowed it.

"No One Is Spared"

Anne's diary more frequently contained somber entries, such as the report that "Children come home from school to find their parents have disappeared." In the evenings, Anne sometimes saw from her window "long lines of good, innocent people, accompanied by crying children, walking on and on, ordered about by a handful of men who bully and beat them until they nearly drop. No one is spared. The sick, the elderly, children, babies and pregnant women—all are marched to their death."[87] Even Mrs. Frank admitted to Miep that she doubted they would survive.

Anne felt "wicked sleeping in a warm bed, while somewhere out there my dearest friends are dropping from exhaustion or being knocked to the ground." In one dream, Hannah appeared, "dressed in rags, her face thin and worn. She looked at me with such sadness and reproach in her enormous eyes that I could read the message in them: 'Oh, Anne, why have you deserted me? Help me, help me, rescue me from this hell!'" Anne later added that "I keep seeing her enormous eyes, and they haunt me."[88]

What had once been the most secure of havens for Anne—the peaceful realm of sleep, to which she could drift off and thereby escape the terror that enveloped her by day—had at last been assaulted by the outside world. The nightmare by day had now created nightmares by night.

The Allies Move Closer

Spring, the season when nature awakens and spreads its message of rebirth and renewal, offered a bright ray of optimism to Anne and the rest. By sticking pins on a map, Otto Frank charted the Allied advance as the troops hammered at Hitler's military machine. By May 1944 everyone in Holland expected a full-scale invasion from England against the coast of France, which had been under German occupation since June 1940. Depending on where the invasion occurred, less than three hundred miles would then separate Amsterdam from its liberators. Anne wrote on

---

Despair Creeps In

No matter how optimistic Anne tried to be, weeks and months confined to the Annex was bound to vent itself in feelings of despair. This entry of May 26, 1944, is illustrative.

"I've asked myself again and again whether it wouldn't have been better if we hadn't gone into hiding, if we were dead now and didn't have to go through this misery, especially so that the others could be spared the burden. But we all shrink from this thought. We still love life, we haven't yet forgotten the voice of nature, and we keep hoping, hoping for . . . everything.

Let something happen soon, even an air raid. Nothing can be more crushing than this anxiety. Let the end come, however cruel; at least then we'll know whether we are to be the victors or the vanquished."

World War II, 1943–1945

Legend:
- Axis occupation
- Allied nations
- Neutral nations
- → Major Allied drives
- ✳ Major battles

Norwegian Sea

North Atlantic Ocean

Murmansk

Narvik

Trondheim

FINLAND

NORWAY

SWEDEN

Gulf of Bothnia

Oslo

Stockholm

Leningrad

USSR

Moscow

North Sea

DENMARK

Hamburg

Baltic Sea

IRELAND

GREAT BRITAIN

London

NETHERLANDS

Antwerp

Berlin

Warsaw

✳ Kursk July 1943

Stalingrad

English Channel

BELGIUM

Battle of the Bulge Dec. 1944

GERMANY

Kiev

Normandy Invasion June 6, 1944

Paris

FRANCE

SWITZERLAND

Vienna

SLOVAKIA

HUNGARY

Budapest

ROMANIA

Bay of Biscay

Rhone Valley Invasion

ITALY

YUGOSLAVIA

Adriatic Sea

BULGARIA

Black Sea

IRAN

PORTUGAL

SPAIN

Madrid

Rome

Anzio Jan. 1944

Cassino Nov. 1943

Salerno Sept. 1943

ALBANIA

GREECE

Aegean Sea

TURKEY

Algiers

Mediterranean Sea

Tunis

Ionian Sea

SICILY

Athens

CYPRUS

SYRIA

Oran

Casablanca

ALGERIA

Sicily Invaded July-August 1943

CRETE

LEBANON

IRAQ

MOROCCO

Kasserine Pass Feb. 1943

✳ TUNISIA

Tripoli

Benghazi

PALESTINE

TRANSJORDAN

SAUDI ARABIA

Cairo

LIBYA

EGYPT

Scale of Miles 500

May 22 that people "are talking about the invasion day and night, debating, making bets and . . . hoping."[89]

By June 5 news reached the Annex that Rome had been occupied by the Americans and that France was being heavily bombarded by Allied aircraft. The invasion could only be days away. However, the eight faced a dilemma. Most of the money they had smuggled in with them had been used, raising serious doubts about how they would survive. "What are we going to live on next month?"[90] wondered Anne. Ever more fervently they prayed that the American and British armies would begin their assault against the French coast.

Anne and Peter

As Anne matured, she began to notice aspects about people she had overlooked. She wondered whether her seeing Peter hurt Margot. "I know I'd be insanely jealous, but Margot just says I shouldn't feel sorry for her,"[91] wrote Anne. Margot did admit to some envy and scribbled her sister a letter in which she stated, "I only feel a bit sorry that I haven't found anyone yet, and am not likely to for the time being, with whom I can discuss my thoughts and feelings."[92]

Others cast furtive glances toward Anne as she wandered into Peter's room. Mrs. van Pels boldly asked, "Can I trust you two up there?" Otto Frank advised Anne to be careful because she was spending so much time alone with Peter. He told his daughter that men normally are more aggressive than women, and that she should stop "necking."[93]

They did not have to worry, for Anne had lost her youthful crush on Peter. Though the two discussed many topics, including sex, marriage, and future occupations, he never shared his deepest feelings, and Anne concluded that Peter was "still a child, emotionally no older than I am."[94]

After examining the matter, Anne concluded that Peter had been "my conquest, and not the other way around." She had created the image that he was sweet and sensitive because she needed someone to talk to, but now he could only be like any other friend. However, he had come to depend too much on Anne. "I honestly don't see any effective way of shaking him off and getting him back on his own two feet,"[95] she wrote on July 15, 1944.

The carefree spirit exhibited in this early photo of Anne disappeared once she and her family were confined in the Annex. Her journal records continual concerns about money, personality conflicts, and being discovered by the Nazis.

More Break-Ins

Of the frequent burglaries in the warehouse, the worst scare took place on April 9, 1944—Easter Sunday. After hearing noises around 9:30 that morning, the four men cautiously left the Annex to investigate. For thirty minutes the others waited, "too scared to think."

When a pale Mr. Frank returned, he told the women to turn off the lights and be quiet, as "we're expecting the police!" He explained that a large panel had been missing from the warehouse door, and when Mr. van Pels saw burglars, he had yelled out to scare them. The would-be burglars then dashed out the door, and the men replaced the panel, but within minutes someone from outside kicked it loose and shone a flashlight through the opening. The four sprinted back to the Annex, fearing that the police had arrived, and huddled with the others to quietly await events.

For an hour nothing happened. At 11:15 they froze, for they heard footsteps slowly advance "in the house, the private office, the kitchen, then . . . on the staircase. All sounds of breathing stopped, eight hearts pounded. Footsteps on the stairs, then a rattling at the bookcase. This moment is indescribable."

Sure that they were about to be captured and hauled away to a concentration camp, Anne blurted out, "Now we're done for." The intruder shook the bookcase twice more, causing such terror that "a shiver went through everyone's body, I heard several sets of teeth chattering, no one said a word." When the footsteps receded, all eight remained where they were, too fearful to move and possibly alert anyone who might still be lurking in the building.

All night they stayed in place, fitfully attempting to get a few moments' rest, but fear would not allow them to let down their guard. Eventually, they started to whisper about the event, and the van Pelses and Dr. Pfeffer wondered whether, since Anne's diary contained names of their helpers, the book should be burned. Anne shot back, "Oh, not my diary; if my diary goes, I go too!"

When a frightened Mrs. van Pels mentioned the possibility of being caught, Anne tried to comfort her by saying, "We must behave like soldiers, Mrs. [van Pels]. If our time has come, well, then, it'll be for Queen and Country, for freedom, truth and justice, as they're always telling us on the radio."

"I Was Ready for Death"

A sleepless night finally ended, and in the morning Miep and Jan informed the residents that a night watchman had discovered the shattered door and reported the break-in. Later, the watchman had accompanied a police officer on the noisy search of the warehouse. Anne could hardly believe that "the police were right at the bookcase, the light was on, and still no one had discovered our hiding place!" Anne mentioned that "That night I really thought I was going to die. I waited for the police and I was ready for death, like a soldier on a battlefield."[96]

In late May another incident further rattled everyone's nerves. Mr. van Hoeven, who had been supplying some of their food, was arrested and taken away. Anne somberly confided to her diary, "What will we do if we're ever . . . no, I mustn't write that down. But the question won't let itself be pushed to the back of my mind today; on the contrary, all the fear I've ever felt is looming before me in all its horror."[97]

As a result, Anne's sleep became more fitful. Alone with her thoughts, she saw herself confined in a dungeon or roaming the streets alone at night. Petrified, Anne imagined that the Nazis "come in the middle of the night to take us away and I crawl under my bed in desperation."[98]

Mr. van Hoeven's arrest worsened an already critical food situation. In late May the residents of the Annex began to skip breakfast, eating hot cereal and bread for lunch, and fried potatoes for dinner, with fruit or vegetables once or twice a week. At times they had only one item to eat for each meal because Miep and Jan were able to purchase a large supply of a particular food. Anne joked about the "food cycles" they endured, switching from spinach to cucumbers to sauerkraut. "It's not much fun when you have to eat, say, sauerkraut every day for lunch and dinner, but when you're hungry enough, you do a lot of things."[99]

The food shortage led to unforeseen problems. A lack of protein and vitamins caused Anne to miss two menstrual periods. Mr. van Pels, driven to desperation by hunger pangs, was caught sneaking sugar, and Otto voiced his displeasure that the van Pelses had kept a larger portion of meat for themselves.

Most harmful, though, was the effect of hunger on people's tempers. Mrs. Frank proclaimed she did not want to see Mr. van Pels's face for two weeks, and Anne exploded at Pfeffer because he hogged so much of the gravy. "All I see around me are dissatisfied and grumpy faces, all I hear are sighs and stifled complaints," Anne

wrote on April 14, 1944. She burst out in exasperation the next month, "How much longer will this increasingly oppressive, unbearable weight press down on us?"[100]

The exuberant Anne felt more like a prisoner. She compared herself to "a songbird whose wings have been ripped off and who keeps hurling itself against the bars of its dark cage. 'Let me out, where there's fresh air and laughter!' a voice within me cries." She longed to "have a really good time for once and to laugh so hard it hurts," and wanted to get outside and ride a bicycle, dance, and walk in the park, to "feel young and know that I'm free."[101]

The Invasion Begins

In the midst of the gloom, the event arrived for which they had anxiously awaited. On June 6, 1944, the eight erupted in joy with the news that the invasion of France had begun. If the Allies could sweep across France and enter Hol-

Jews in Chains

The Easter break-in was the scariest experience to date in the Annex. It reminded Anne of her religion's heritage, as she mentions in her April 11, 1944, entry.

"We've been strongly reminded of the fact that we're Jews in chains, chained to one spot, without any rights, but with a thousand obligations. We must put our feelings aside; we must be brave and strong, bear discomfort without complaint, do whatever is in our power and trust in God. One day this terrible war will be over. The time will come when we'll be people again and not just Jews!"

land, the members of the Annex believed they would be free before the end of the year. Anne confided to her diary, "Oh, Kitty, the best part about the invasion is that I have the feeling that friends are on the way."[102] Margot even gushed that they might be back in school by September.

On July 21 they learned that members of the German opposition had attempted to assassinate Hitler. If the Allies could not reach them, maybe the German people would overturn the Nazi government and restore peace to Europe. All they had to do was avoid detection, and Mr. Frank believed that they would have to hold out only until early October.

With the world about her in constant turmoil and the war approaching its climax, Anne began to piece together the puzzle comprising her personality and future. Her comments in the spring of 1944 exuded more confidence, and her goals crystallized. In June she declared that "Modern women want the right to be completely independent," and she stated that they deserved to be respected as much as soldiers: "Women, who struggle and suffer pain to ensure the continuation of the human race, make much tougher and more courageous soldiers than all those big-mouthed freedom-fighting heroes put together!"[103]

Anne felt ever more strongly that she wanted to be a famous writer, visit scenic locations, and meet important people.

One day in July she helped strip pea pods, a job she detested, and commented later that "Every string I pulled made me more certain that I never, ever, want to be just a housewife!" While she thought her writing was good, she experienced moments of doubt about its importance. She wrote that "sometimes I seriously doubt whether anyone will ever be interested in this drivel." She added later that "*My* (italics hers) diaries certainly won't be of much use"[104] to the Dutch government after the war.

Anne claimed that the children faced a tougher struggle in the Annex than the adults because they had yet to live their lives, while the adults had at least experienced something. Just when teenagers began to form their ideals and goals, a war started by adults knocked their world spinning. She claimed that it was "difficult in times like these: ideals, dreams and cherished hopes rise within us, only to be crushed by grim reality. It's a wonder I haven't abandoned all my ideals, they seem so absurd and impractical." She then wrote the words for which she is most noted. "Yet I cling to them because I still believe, in spite of everything, that people are truly good at heart."[105]

Committed to paper shortly before the beginning of August 1944, this belief would be put to a horrible test within days. The time in the Annex, sheltered and safe, was at an end.

7 "Extermination Was . . . the Objective"

Friday, August 4, began like any other day in the Annex. A ringing alarm awakened everyone at 6:45 A.M. After eating his meager breakfast, Otto Frank walked upstairs to Peter's room to help him with his English lesson.

The serenity ended in less than four hours. At 10:30 A.M., five Dutch Nazis led by Karl Silberbauer stormed into the front office where Miep worked and pointed their pistols at the startled secretary. Silberbauer warned Miep, "Stay put. Don't move."[106] Silberbauer, who obviously knew that people were living in the Annex, stepped toward Victor Kugler's office while his cohorts spread throughout the building. A frightened Johannes Kleiman looked at Miep and muttered, "Miep, I think the time has come."[107]

The Arrest

When Silberbauer ordered Kugler to open the bookcase, Kugler attempted to divert his attention by claiming, "But there's only a bookcase there!"[108] Silberbauer angrily pulled open the bookcase, stuck his pistol in Kugler's back, and yelled at him to walk upstairs.

Kugler and the five Nazis entered one of the Franks' rooms, where Mrs. Frank

stood with Anne. The officers gruffly ordered the two petrified women to raise their hands into the air, and while four men guarded them at gunpoint a fifth dashed up to the van Pelses' area. The officer shouted at Mr. and Mrs. van Pels and Dr. Pfeffer to stand still, then walked to the adjoining room to get Otto and Peter. The officers took the five downstairs, where Otto saw his wife and daughters waiting with hands raised.

The van Pelses, the Franks, and Dr. Pfeffer entered the office, and Miep "could tell from their footsteps that they were coming down like beaten dogs."[109] Silberbauer demanded they hand over any valuables, such as money and jewelry. Looking for something in which to place the items, Silberbauer grabbed Otto Frank's briefcase and thoughtlessly dumped out its contents—replacing Anne's diary and loose pages of entries with the loot he had demanded.

Silberbauer allowed each captive to pack one bag before taking everyone outside to a waiting vehicle. As the eight left the room at gunpoint, they walked directly over the scattered papers of Anne's diary entries, now littering the floor like so many pieces of trash.

Before leaving, Silberbauer harshly asked Miep, "Aren't you ashamed that you are helping Jewish garbage?" Miep noticed his Viennese accent and stated that she had been born in the Austrian city. Silberbauer decided not to arrest her, but warned her not to flee: "From personal sympathy . . . from me personally, you can stay. But God help you if you run away. Then we take your husband." [110]

Taken to Prison

The eight, plus Kugler and Kleiman, filed into a van that transported them to the German Gestapo headquarters, where they were confined in a large room. Mr. Frank tried to apologize to Kugler and Kleiman, who now faced imprisonment and death for their actions, but Kleiman answered without hesitation, "Don't give it another thought. It was up to me, and I wouldn't have done it differently." [111]

The next day the eight Annex residents were transferred to Weteringschans Prison, where they waited for three days until the train that would carry them to a concentration camp had been prepared. Within a brief two-month span, they had plummeted from the heights of hope with the Allied invasion, to the depths of despair with their seizure.

The Diary Is Saved

After their friends had been led away, Miep and Jan returned to the Annex to see what remained. Drawers had been pulled out of dressers, closets emptied, and clothing, books, and other items tossed everywhere. Out of the mess, though, Miep instantly recognized something. "On the floor, amidst the chaos of papers and books, my eye lit on the little red-orange checkered, cloth-bound diary that Anne had received from her father on her thirteenth birthday." Miep carefully retrieved it and other papers of Anne's and locked them in the bottom drawer of her desk. She told Bep, "I'll keep everything safe for Anne until she comes back." [112] Fortunately for posterity, Miep recovered these precious writings, for a few days later a German truck pulled up and workers removed what was left in the Annex.

Because of poor health, Johannes Kleiman was released after only a few weeks in jail. The Nazis sent Victor Kugler to a forced labor camp, but he escaped after a few months, returned to Amsterdam, and spent the duration of the war hiding in his own house.

Who Turned Them In?

Despite an exhaustive investigation conducted after the war by the Netherlands State Institute for War Documentation, no one is sure who informed authorities that a group of Jews lived in the Annex. Most suspicions focus on the warehouse worker, van Maaren. Hired in 1943, he sometimes acted strangely. Before going home for the night, he would set little traps for the Jews he apparently believed to be concealed on the premises. Frequently, for example, he left pencils balancing on table edges or he sprinkled the floor with flour. Pencils on the floor, or floury footprints, would have served to bolster an accusation.

When researchers for the institute questioned Silberbauer, he could not remember much about the case. "There

Jews are forced onto trains headed for concentration camps. The occupants of the Annex rode two such trains: the first took them to the Westerbork detainment camp, the second took them to the death camp at Auschwitz.

were so many betrayals during those years,"[113] he explained, adding that nothing in particular made this one any more special than the countless others. Whoever the informant had been received the normal reward for such a deed—$1.40 per Jew, or a grand total of $11.20.

The Train to Westerbork

Early on August 8 the Franks, the van Pelses, and Dr. Pfeffer were taken to Central Station in Amsterdam for the train ride to their first concentration camp. The camp to which they were shipped in eastern Holland —Westerbork—had been busily processing Dutch Jews since 1942. Although inmates were forced to do factory work, the facility operated mainly as an interim holding point until arrangements could be made to transfer Jews to Auschwitz or to Sobibor, death camps located deep in Germany or in Poland. By the time Anne Frank arrived,

more than a hundred thousand Jews had passed through Westerbork on their way to the gas chambers.

According to Ronnie Goldstein-van Cleef, another Jewish inmate at Westerbork, "The Franks were pretty depressed. They had had the feeling that nothing could happen to them. They were very close to each other."[114]

Though far from the worst that the Franks would experience, Westerbork contained its own share of horrors. Awakened early so that they could be at work by 5:00 A.M., the adults and teens broke up old batteries for usable parts. Children worked in a cable shop or completed other chores.

Sitting at long tables with people assigned to the same task, Anne and Margot could at least chat with others, but the job was no easy matter. After prying open the batteries with a chisel and hammer, they had to reach in and remove a sticky, tarlike substance, along with some carbon bars and metal caps, and place these materials in separate baskets.

Rumors flooded the camp that since the Russian army neared from the east while the American and British armies closed in from the west, liberation was within sight. Though the German army was in retreat on all fronts, Anne and the other inmates were mistaken in their hopes.

What most terrified every Jew in Westerbork was the thought that they might be shipped to extermination camps in the east before the Allies arrived to free them. According to Janny Brandes-Brilleslijper, who was about Anne's age, whenever inmates heard that another transport had pulled in to ship Jews east, "we were all terribly frightened. Everyone tried to avoid the transport." Inmates faked serious illness in hopes of remaining in Westerbork, because, "We knew that Auschwitz was a death camp."[115] They realized that even one more day at Westerbork offered the opportunity that they might be saved by the Allies, rather than face the nightmare of Auschwitz.

The Franks Are Taken to Auschwitz

In early September the final train to leave Westerbork pulled in to pick up a thousand Jews for Auschwitz. Unfortunately for the eight former residents of the Annex, they were among the 498 men, 442 women, and 79 children selected for this last train out of Westerbork. With the Allied armies only 120 miles away, on September 3 armed guards shoved the eight into a boxcar normally used to ship cattle, then bolted shut the door. Packed in tightly with 70 other inmates, the Franks stood on straw-covered wooden floors and

---

Fear of the Transports

Rachel van Amerongen-Frankfoorder powerfully describes the fear that coursed through every Jewish woman when a transport pulled into Westerbork. This recollection is from Willy Lindwer's The Last Seven Months of Anne Frank.

"It was always very terrible when a transport arrived. . . . You knew, very well, where they were going, and that it always meant death.

I saw that clearly, and I think most people realized it. No one dared to say it out loud. But everyone was eager to stay in the Netherlands as long as possible.

In the evenings, there was an announcement of the names of those who would have to go, and there was always the fear that your name might be included. You were always thinking, Oh, I hope the liberation will come soon. Because we did get news that the liberation was imminent. It was a race against time, and we all hoped for it."

shivered from the cold wind that whipped through cracks in the wooden walls.

Conditions in each boxcar for the three-day trip to Auschwitz were horrendous. One small window located near the ceiling provided meager light during the day, while at night a solitary candle in a can that hung from above offered even less illumination. The air soon turned foul with so many sweating bodies, and as the journey wound through the country, people had to urinate and defecate where they stood. Since the door remained tightly shut—even when the train stopped for hours at a time—men, women, and children hoped to be near a crack in the wall to receive some fresh air.

With no room to lie down, Anne and Margot leaned against their parents when they needed a restful moment. As the first day lengthened into days two and three without sleep or food, the hungry, cold

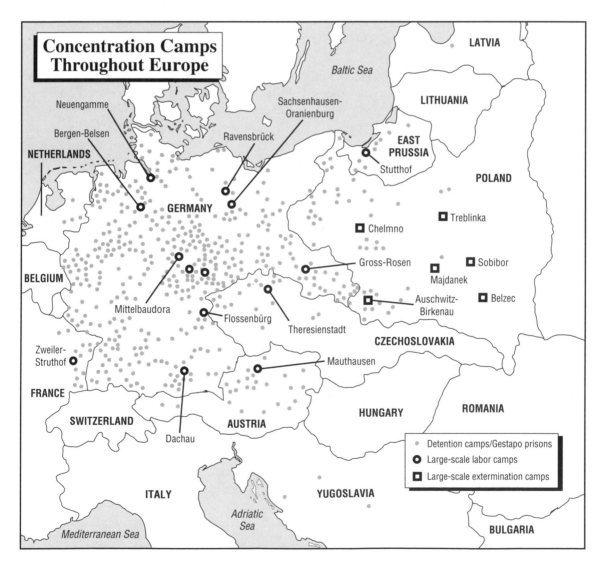

Concentration Camps Throughout Europe

Anne and her family suffered intolerable conditions in a boxcar for three days while being transported to Auschwitz. Many Jews, however, never survived the train ride to the concentration camps.

people turned irritable. Janny Brandes-Brilleslijper mentioned that "the kindest, gentlest people become aggressive when they've stood for a long time. And you get tired—so terribly tired—that you just want to lean against something, or if possible, even if only for a minute, to sit down on the straw."[116]

The trek from Westerbork ended in the middle of the night. The train pulled up to the gates of Auschwitz-Birkenau in Poland, a death camp ready to receive another shipment of victims to add to its already ghastly total of 2 million Jews gassed.

Arrival at Auschwitz

After the train jerked to a stop, the doors grated open and uniformed soldiers, armed with whips and restraining snarling dogs on leashes, screamed for everyone to climb out. As guards kicked and shoved them along, the Jews stepped from dark boxcars into an eerie bluish haze produced from giant spotlights. A booming voice over a loudspeaker ordered them to "put down your luggage, women to one side, men to the other side. Women and

children who can't walk, go to the cars that are waiting for you." Petrified at the ghastly sounds and strange sights, Anne, Margot, and the rest lined up and walked toward the camp like numbed robots. "It was inhumane, degrading, how they guarded us with whips, with dogs,"[117] said Lenie de Jong, who rode in the same boxcar with Anne Frank.

The long line stumbled through Auschwitz's gate bearing the inscription "ARBEIT MACHT FREI," German for "Work brings freedom." They continued past watchtowers manned by guards with machine guns and noticed barbed wire and electrified poles everywhere. Though weary from the arduous train ride, they had to keep moving or face beating, for the guards constantly shouted at them to go "faster, faster, faster."[118]

The Jews walked toward an officer who divided the arrivals into two groups by quietly pointing to the left or right with a baton. Dr. Josef Mengele, nicknamed the "Angel of Death" for his hideous role in exterminating Jewish prisoners, determined who would live and who would die with a flick of his wrist. The 549 sent to the left—the elderly, the ill, and anyone under age fifteen—died in Auschwitz's gas chambers

At left, a sign above a concentration camp reads: "Work brings freedom."
Many concentration camps offered such false hope to arriving Jews. In
truth, work kept the prisoners busy until they could be murdered and sent
to crematoria like the ones shown at right.

the next day; members of the group to the right would live as long as they were healthy enough to work. Since Anne had turned fifteen a few months earlier, she was spared, but Dr. Mengele sent the sickly looking Hermann van Pels to the left. The next day, Mr. van Pels became the first of the Annex residents to perish. He was gassed to death in chambers disguised as showers; his remains, along with those of the others who died, were cremated in one of Auschwitz's enormous ovens, or crematoria.

After this "selection," the first of the ghastly rituals conducted each day to determine who would perish in the gas chambers, guards split the survivors into two groups. Otto, Peter, and Dr. Pfeffer headed for the men's barracks in Auschwitz, while Anne, Margot, Mrs. Frank, and Mrs. van Pels were led into the women's barracks at the adjoining camp of Birkenau. As the fe-

males walked away, Anne and Margot vainly tried to get a glimpse of the men. They would never again see their father.

Along with the other women, Anne was taken to large offices where a female worker grabbed her left arm, harshly twisted it around, and tattooed a number by jabbing with a needle. Other workers then forced open her mouth to see if there were any gold teeth or gold fillings. These would be extracted after her death. Gold obtained in this way was melted down, formed into ingots, and used to help pay the costs of the war.

The girls next walked into a second hall, where they had to undress and toss their clothing onto a huge pile. As they stood, painfully embarrassed by the forced nakedness, they suffered the humiliation of having every particle of hair shaved from their bodies. Anne, who had loved fixing her long black hair and considered it one of her best features, suffered with silent tears as a camp worker shaved her head bald.

The females then headed outside, where workers handed them threadbare clothing. Lenie de Jong was given "a torn pajama top, some kind of skirt, and nothing underneath, absolutely nothing." Guards lined up the shabbily dressed women in precise rows and conducted a roll call. "We were a sight to see with those bald heads,"[119] stated de Jong. Guards finally dished out some food—one can of brownish liquid and one piece of bread for the entire row—before leading the women to their barracks.

Auschwitz-Birkenau

The Franks quickly realized that Westerbork was a rest camp compared to Birkenau. Edith Frank, Anne, and Margot were placed in *Frauenblock* (women's barracks) #29, a wooden structure filled with wide cots where seven or eight women slept huddled together. That first night a

Arrival at Auschwitz

The arrival at Auschwitz was such an unforgettable experience that years later, the painful memories lingered. In David A. Adler's We Remember the Holocaust, *Ernest Honig recalls his entry to the camp.*

"It was early evening when the train stopped and the doors opened. As I came off the train, I saw on the left huge chimneys belching forth thick black smoke. There was a strange smell, like burning the feathers off a chicken before it was cooked. . . .

My brother and I were standing next to each other. We wondered what that could be. One of us said, 'Maybe a factory. Maybe they're making rubber. Maybe that's where we'll be working.' But it occurred to me, as it must have to my brother, that maybe they were burning people."

Prisoners peer from a boxcar window as they travel to Auschwitz.

woman left the barracks to use the latrine and was shot by the guards. She lay on the ground all night, groaning in pain, but Anne and the other newer inmates were warned by those who had been in camp a while to stay in their cots, or else they would also be shot. When morning roll call sounded, the woman was dead.

To the shouts of "Out of the barracks, roll call," Anne and the others clambered out of bed at 3:30 A.M. As Janny Brandes-Brilleslijper recalled, to avoid a guard's wrath most "jumped out of the bunks and ran outside. We were kicked out of the barracks by the women guards, the barrack *Kapos*."[120] On the way out to line up for roll call, lukewarm coffee was poured into their food pans, which some girls used to clean their teeth or rinse their faces.

As the days passed, the girls tried to remain near the same friends during the lengthy roll calls so that they could lean on each other for a bit of rest. Anne always stood near Margot, and they sometimes waited for hours as the guards laboriously counted the two thousand in-

mates. If the number counted did not agree with the total the guards expected, they started counting again. To prevent any mishap, other guards stood by with dogs on leashes. "God help you if they got loose," Janny Brandes-Brilleslijper told an interviewer, "because they bit, those nasty animals."[121]

Following roll call, the Jews were forced to work at meaningless tasks, normally imposed to humiliate them. Most had to carry huge stones from one side of camp to the other. Others, under the careful watch of whip-toting *kapos*, lugged boulders from rock pits to hilltops.

The food, mostly bread with occasional helpings of butter, was barely sufficient to maintain minimal health. Anne was chosen by four other girls to divide the daily hunks of black bread. According to an inmate, she performed this job "so well and fairly that there was none of the usual grumbling."[122] Each woman, however, suffered as a result of the meager diet. Lack of vitamins produced blisters and sores in their mouths and on their tongues; stom-

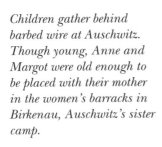

Children gather behind barbed wire at Auschwitz. Though young, Anne and Margot were old enough to be placed with their mother in the women's barracks in Birkenau, Auschwitz's sister camp.

Death on a Large Scale

In her book Tell Them We Remember: The Story of the Holocaust, *Susan D. Bachrach explains how the Nazis killed on a large scale.*

"A guard closed and locked the steel door [to the gas chamber]. In some killing centers, carbon monoxide was piped into the chamber. In others, camp guards threw 'Zyklon B' pellets down an air shaft. Zyklon B was a highly poisonous insecticide also used to kill rats and insects.

Usually within minutes after entering the gas chambers, everyone inside was dead from lack of oxygen. Under guard, prisoners were forced to haul the corpses to a nearby room, where they removed hair, gold teeth, and fillings. The bodies were burned in ovens in the crematoria or buried in mass graves."

Canisters of Zyklon B gas pellets. Germans used this deadly insecticide to kill millions of Jews.

ach cramps and diarrhea afflicted them; few of the women menstruated. Conditions so deteriorated that Anne, Margot, and even Mrs. Frank became adept at stealing food from containers earmarked for elsewhere or from supply rooms.

For a time, Anne and Margot were placed in the sick barracks because they had developed scabies, a severe skin disease caused by mites that produced intense itching. To help the two emerge alive, Mrs. Frank and Lenie de Jong dug a hole under the barracks and shoved bread through to the sick girls. Another ill inmate, Ronnie

Goldstein-van Cleef, sang to them to lift their spirits. "The Frank girls looked terrible, their hands and bodies covered with spots and sores from scabies," she explained. "They were in a very bad way; pitiful —that's how I thought of them. There wasn't any clothing. They had taken everything from us. We were all lying there, naked, under some kind of blankets." [123]

The terrors of Birkenau caused Janny Brandes-Brillesliper to compare life in camp to "that of a mouse, who runs through the house, chased by everyone—the panic it feels when it can't find the hole it came out of." Rats scampered about the grounds and barracks. The daily "selections" to determine who headed for the gas chambers unnerved even the hardiest inmates. After morning roll call the females had to return to their barracks, undress, and then walk out one by one as their names were called so Dr. Mengele or one of his guards could closely inspect each woman for signs of illness. Rachel van Amerongen-Frankfoorder endured these ordeals in constant fright, for "every scratch, every pimple, might mean death to you."[124]

Anne walked and worked among the dead, for when someone died, the body would be placed outside the barracks, where it remained on the ground until a work detail came along—"carts with corpses, pulled by moving corpses, skeletons, with ropes over their shoulders," as one survivor explained—and took it away for cremation. Ronnie Goldstein-van Cleef stated that the Frank girls tried to avoid noticing the dead but "were just as afraid and nervous as I was, and they were apprehensive, just as all of us were. The emotional shock at the existence of something like that—they felt that as well."[125]

Especially haunting to Anne was the sight of other girls, staring out from hopeless eyes, as they numbly plodded toward the gas chambers, for as Rachel van Amerongen-Frankfoorder explained, "extermination was, of course, the objective of Auschwitz and Birkenau."[126] A woman who had stood near Anne during one instance recalled:

I can still see [Anne] standing at the door and looking down the camp street as a herd of naked Gypsy girls was driven by to the crematory, and Anne watched them go and cried. And she cried also when we marched past the Hungarian children who had already been waiting half a day in the rain in front of the gas chambers because it was not yet their turn. And Anne nudged me and said, "Look, look. Their eyes. . . ."[127]

Mrs. Frank tried to never let Anne or Margot out of her sight. If they had to use the latrine, she walked with them in case a guard strolled by. Lenie de Jong claimed that Mrs. Frank "tried very hard to keep her children alive, to keep them with her, to protect them."[128]

Anne and Margot Leave Auschwitz

On October 28, 1944, with the Russian army and freedom only sixty miles away, Anne and Margot were shipped out of Auschwitz for another concentration camp farther from the Allies. After being stripped for another selection and ordered to get on the transport, Anne took Margot's arm and helped her forward. A woman standing next to the horrified Mrs. Frank said, "Anne turned her serene face toward us; then they were led away. It was impossible to see what happened behind the light, and Mrs. Frank cried, 'The children! My God! My God!'"[129] The mother would see her daughters no more.

Chapter

8 "Now Anne's Voice Would Never Be Lost"

The train bearing Anne and Margot pulled into Bergen-Belsen, a concentration camp in northern Germany, on October 30. The girls, who had so depended on their father and mother but were now on their own, had to walk a few miles from the train station to the camp. After a brief stay in makeshift tents, Anne and Margot moved into a barracks peopled with disease-ridden inmates. A woman who had first met the Franks at Westerbork, Rachel van Amerongen-Frankfoorder, spotted the two girls and was shocked at what she saw. "The Frank girls were almost unrecognizable since their hair had been cut off. . . . And they were cold."[130]

Anne Is Reunited with an Old Friend

Anne experienced fleeting moments of happiness in Bergen-Belsen, even though she and Margot waged a continuous battle against ill health. Anne and other young females visited with a large group of Dutch children, incarcerated while the Nazis tried to determine whether they were Jewish. They shared stories and laughter with the youngsters, and according to Janny Brandes-Brilleslijper, also now confined in

Bergen-Belsen, "We acted toward them like anxious mothers."[131]

Most astonishing was that Anne encountered Hannah, her close friend from school days. Though living in a barracks on the other side of barbed wire, Hannah learned that Anne, Margot, and Mrs. van Pels were close by. One night, though she could have been shot if caught by a guard, she called across the wire to Mrs. van Pels, who replied, "Yes, yes, wait a minute, I'll go to get Anne. I can't get Margot; she is very, very ill and is in bed."

When Anne stumbled to the barbed wire Hannah almost cried, for the girl she gazed at was hardly the vivacious Anne of the past. "She was a broken girl," stated Hannah, who added that Anne "immediately began to cry, and she told me, 'I don't have any parents anymore.'"

Hannah and Anne stared at each other through the wire, and for long moments did nothing but cry. Anne told Hannah that "We don't have anything at all to eat here, almost nothing, and we are cold; we don't have any clothes and I've gotten very thin and they shaved my hair."

The next night Hannah attempted to toss a few crackers and cookies across the wire to Anne, but her effort met only loud screams from the other side. Anne explained that "the woman standing next to

Allied medics were often unable to save all the Jews who survived until liberation. Here, a prisoner at the Bergen-Belsen concentration camp slowly dies after being freed.

me caught it, and she won't give it back to me."[132] Hannah successfully tried again a few days later, which was the final time the two former schoolmates saw each other.

The Frank Girls Weaken

In some ways, Bergen-Belsen proved to be worse than Birkenau. At Birkenau sickly people quickly disappeared into the ovens, but death lingered at Bergen-Belsen. Inmates lay dying in their bunks from typhus and other serious illnesses, slowly wasting away before the eyes of their fellow prisoners. When someone finally succumbed, prisoners were forced to wrap the body in a blanket and drag it to a large pit, where they tossed it on top of other bodies.

Anne told Janny Brandes-Brilleslijper that the countless lice that infested her clothing so horrified her that she discarded the items. The young girl had but one thin blanket to shield her from winter's biting cold, and under such conditions it was in-

evitable that she would weaken. Rachel van Amerongen-Frankfoorder recalled that "The Frank girls were so emaciated. They looked terrible. . . . It was clear that they had typhus."[133] Caused by infections created by tiny parasites called mites, typhus reduced its victims to hollow shells of their former selves. Both girls, with their sunken cheeks and frail bodies, reminded Rachel of skeletons.

Unfortunately, Anne and Margot shared a bunk in one of the worst places in the barracks—directly near the entrance, where they received harsh drafts whenever the door opened. Anne or Margot constantly pled with the others to "Close the door, close the door," but everyone knew that they were very near death. Rachel said that their "voices became weaker every day."[134]

Anne Frank Dies

The symptoms of typhus—weight loss, apathy, and hopelessness—soon overwhelmed

Anne and Margot. Anne struggled to help her weaker sister, but she could do little but offer feeble words of solace. Sometime in late February or early March 1945, Margot lapsed into a coma, fell out of her bunk onto the stone floor, and, too weak to get up, died where she lay. Within a day or so Anne, broken in spirit, succumbed to the disease.

Following the usual procedure, workers dragged the lifeless forms of Anne and Margot to the pit and added the bodies to the heap of remains. The girl who had injected vitality into every endeavor now shared an unmarked grave with her sister and hundreds of nameless victims. Ironically, within five weeks British soldiers liberated Bergen-Belsen. Anne had lost her race with death by the narrowest of margins.

Friedrich Pfeffer was transferred from Auschwitz to Neuengamme concentration camp in northern Germany. He died, most probably from disease, on December 20, 1944. Seventeen days later, on January 6,

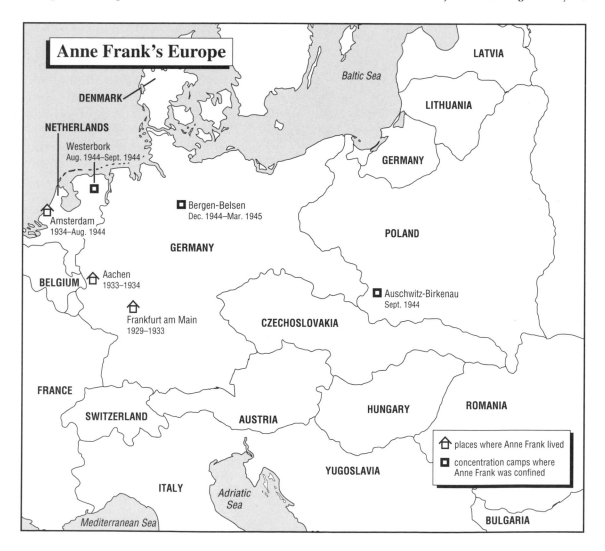

Anne Frank's Europe

- Baltic Sea
- LATVIA
- DENMARK
- LITHUANIA
- NETHERLANDS
- Westerbork Aug. 1944–Sept. 1944
- GERMANY
- Bergen-Belsen Dec. 1944–Mar. 1945
- Amsterdam 1934–Aug. 1944
- POLAND
- GERMANY
- Aachen 1933–1934
- BELGIUM
- Auschwitz-Birkenau Sept. 1944
- Frankfurt am Main 1929–1933
- CZECHOSLOVAKIA
- FRANCE
- HUNGARY
- ROMANIA
- SWITZERLAND
- AUSTRIA
- YUGOSLAVIA
- places where Anne Frank lived
- concentration camps where Anne Frank was confined
- ITALY
- Adriatic Sea
- BULGARIA
- Mediterranean Sea

1945, Edith Frank died in Auschwitz, three weeks before the Russian army arrived and freed the remaining prisoners. After accompanying Anne Frank to Bergen-Belsen, Mrs. van Pels was transferred to Buchenwald in Germany, and finally to the concentration camp at Theresienstadt in Czechoslovakia. She died of disease in the spring of 1945. The seventh member of the Annex to die, Peter van Pels, survived until shortly before the war's end. After being transferred from Auschwitz to Mauthausen camp in Austria, Peter died on May 5, 1945, just three days before the war ended.

Only Otto Frank survived the horrors of confinement, receiving his freedom when Russian forces swept into Auschwitz in late January 1945. Of the 1,019 people who had left Westerbork with Anne and her family five months earlier, 45 men and 82 women survived.

Otto Frank Returns to Amsterdam

As soon as the Russian army freed the inmates at Auschwitz on January 27, 1945, Otto Frank hurried to the adjoining women's camp at Birkenau to search for Edith. The news that his wife had died only a few weeks earlier and that his daughters had been taken away devastated the man.

Since war still raged in the Netherlands, Otto could not start his return voyage until March 5, when he boarded a train bound for the Soviet Union port of Odessa on the Black Sea. While on the train, Otto met another concentration camp survivor, Elfriede Geiringer-Markovits. The two embarked on the *Monoway*, a ship that took them to Mar-

seille, France. After arriving in France on May 27, Otto and Elfriede parted and Otto headed by train and truck to Amsterdam, which he reached on June 3.

That same day Miep looked out her window to see Mr. Frank walking up the steps. After an emotional greeting, Otto said, "Miep, Edith is not coming back." [135] He explained that he knew nothing about his daughters other than they had been shipped to Bergen-Belsen, but hoped that one of the relief agencies in Amsterdam could find word about Anne and Margot. Mr. Frank accepted Miep and Jan's offer to stay with them for as long as he liked.

Otto placed inquiries in various newspapers, trying to obtain information about his daughters. Two months later the Red Cross informed him that Janny Brandes-Brilleslijper, Anne's fellow inmate, had visited the organization's office to check the lists of survivors. When Janny spotted the names of Anne and Margot Frank, she placed a mark indicating that they had died. Otto wanted to hear the news directly from Janny, so he visited her at her home that summer. When she confirmed that his daughters were dead, Janny said, "He took it very hard." [136]

Otto Receives the Diary

When Otto returned to his business in Amsterdam from the visit to Janny, he muttered, "Miep, Margot and Anne are not coming back." After a moment of silence, Otto walked into his office to be alone. Miep gave him some time to cope with his grief, then unlocked her desk drawer, removed the unread diary, and walked into her former employer's office. As she

The Diary Becomes Known

Dr. Jan Romein's article brought public attention to Anne's diary. In his article, which was reprinted by the Netherlands State Institute for War Documentation in its The Diary of Anne Frank: The Critical Edition, *Dr. Romein attempted to explain the diary's importance.*

"By chance a diary written during the war years has come into my possession. The Netherlands State Institute for War Documentation already holds some two hundred similar diaries, but I should be very much surprised if there were another as lucid, as intelligent, and at the same time as natural. This one made me forget the present and its many calls to duty for a whole evening as I read it from beginning to end. . . .

Having arrived here at the age of four from Germany, she was able within ten years to write enviably pure and simple Dutch, and showed an insight into the failings of human nature—her own not excepted—so infallible that it would have astonished one in an adult, let alone in a child. At the same time she also highlighted the infinite possibilities of human nature, reflected in humor, tenderness, and love."

handed the papers to Mr. Frank, Miep said, "Here is your daughter Anne's legacy to you." She then left. A short time later Miep answered the telephone to hear Mr. Frank's request, "Miep, please see to it that I'm not disturbed."[137]

Anne's perceptive observations and comments amazed Otto Frank, who concluded that while he thought they shared a close relationship, he had never truly grasped her personality while she lived. In subsequent days he typed portions of the diary for close friends and for his mother, and frequently he emerged from his office and gushed, "Miep, you should hear this description that Anne wrote here! Who'd have imagined how vivid her imagination was all the while?"[138] Otto urged her to read Anne's diary, but each time Miep po-

litely refused because she did not want to reopen old wounds.

Mr. Frank edited Anne's two versions of her diary—the one she originally started and the revised version, which she had hoped the Dutch government would publish after the war—into a third draft. He included most of what Anne wrote, but omitted sensitive passages that dealt with sex and Anne's harsh feelings toward Edith.

Gradually, Otto hosted weekly gatherings of acquaintances who had survived the Holocaust, and at one session he mentioned Anne's diary. One friend, Dr. Werner Cahn, asked to read portions, and the diary so impressed him that he urged a reluctant Otto to publish the book. Eventually, Cahn received permission to show parts of the diary to a Dutch historian, Dr.

Jan Romein, who on April 3, 1946, published an article in a Dutch newspaper proclaiming its importance and beauty. Romein joined the ever-lengthening list of people trying to coax Otto to publish Anne's diary, arguing that Otto had a duty to history to take the step so that such a horrendous event as the Holocaust would never again occur.

Finally, Otto Frank gave his permission to have a limited publication of fifteen hundred copies printed. Titled *Het Achterhuis* (Dutch for *The Secret Annex*), the book appeared in June 1947 to glowing reviews. Three years later the book was translated and published in Germany and France, followed in 1952 by *Anne Frank: The Diary of a Young Girl*, which appeared in England and the United States. Eleanor Roosevelt, the widow of the wartime president and an esteemed world figure in her own right, wrote the introduction to the U.S. version and called the diaries "one of the wisest and most moving commentaries on war and its impact on human beings" [139] she had ever read.

As the book grew in popularity, Otto pestered Miep to read Anne's thoughts. She continued to hold off for a time, thinking that the memories might be too painful, but under his persistence she finally collapsed. Miep picked up the book one day when she could read it alone, and did not put it down until she had finished:

> When I had read the last word, I didn't feel the pain I'd anticipated. I was glad I'd read it at last. The emptiness in my heart was eased. So much had been lost, but now Anne's voice would never be lost. My young friend had left a remarkable legacy to the world. [140]

Miep was also pleased that she had not read the diary directly after retrieving it from the Annex floor. Since Anne wrote about the various people who helped them, Miep would have destroyed the book to protect them from arrest in case the diary fell into the wrong hands. A literary treasure was thus spared for future generations.

In 1955 the play based on Anne's book opened in New York City. Written by noted Hollywood screenwriters Albert Hackett and his wife, Frances Goodrich, the play captivated audiences and garnered both the 1956 Tony Award for best drama and the 1956 Pulitzer Prize for drama.

The play premiered in the Netherlands in November 1956, one month after stunning audiences in Germany into complete silence with its graphic portrayal of the damage to people, especially youth, inflicted by Hitler and his Nazis. A German critic wrote, "In Düsseldorf, people did not even go out during the intermission. They sat in their seats as if afraid of the lights outside, shamed to face each other." [141]

The Diary Is Attacked

Unfortunately, Anne Frank's invaluable story suffered from controversy. American novelist Meyer Levin had penned an earlier version of the play after receiving permission from Otto Frank. Anne's father, however, rejected the work because Levin incorrectly portrayed the Frank family as Orthodox Jews. An angry Levin sued Otto Frank for breaking a contract and the Hacketts for copying his material. In 1959 Levin agreed to drop the issue for $15,000.

A challenge of another kind emerged in 1958 from Germans sympathetic to the Nazis. Lothat Stielau, a German teacher, asserted that the diary was forged and that the perpetrators of the hoax "have also raised our own hackles quite a bit."[142] Otto Frank sued Stielau, who eventually settled out of court.

In the 1980s, after a thorough examination, the Netherlands State Forensic Science Laboratory announced that the diary had, indeed, been written by Anne Frank. The glue used in the book itself, the style of paper, and the ink Anne wrote with were of the types normally found in the Netherlands during the war years, and an exhaustive comparison of the handwriting in the diary and samples of notes and letters written by Anne in school proved beyond doubt that no one but Anne Frank had penned the words attributed to her.

Even this set of proofs did not silence the book's critics. Nazi sympathizers as late as 1990 claimed that the diary was fake.

One book titled *Anne Frank—The Big Fraud*, boldly stated that "Millions of schoolchildren have been forced and are still being forced to read this fake . . . and now it turns out that it is the product of a New York scriptwriter in collaboration with the girl's father!"[143]

As the years passed, most of the people involved in hiding the Franks died. Johannes Kleiman died in 1959. After moving to Toronto in 1955, Victor Kugler died in 1981, while Bep Voskuijl passed away two years later. Miep and Jan Gies lived a long life together in Amsterdam until 1993, when Jan died. As of this writing, Miep Gies still lives quietly in Amsterdam, honored by her nation as one of its heroes.

In 1952 Mr. Frank moved out of Miep and Jan's apartment to be near his mother in Switzerland. The following year he returned to Amsterdam, where he

Otto Frank edited the diary and notebooks that made up his daughter's journal. He then oversaw its publication.

The building that housed the Secret Annex is now operated as a museum called the Anne Frank House. Each year, the museum attracts thousands of visitors who wish to learn more about the Holocaust.

married Elfriede Geiringer-Markovits, whom he had met on the train ride from Auschwitz.

The couple settled in Switzerland, where Otto retired from business to devote full time to answering the thousands of pieces of mail he received each year. Schoolchildren around the world wrote lengthy letters to him, and he carefully responded to each one.

On August 19, 1980, Otto Frank passed away in Birsfelden, Switzerland, at the age of 91. As stipulated in his will, all Anne's papers were donated to the State of Netherlands.

The Impact of Anne Frank

Anne Frank's story has profoundly affected people through the years. Since it was first published, the diary has been translated into fifty-five languages, and more than 20 million copies have been sold. Nations have honored the teenage girl in various ways. In the town where she died, Bergen, Germany, an elementary school bears her name. Israel planted the Anne Frank Forest, where ten thousand trees memorialize her name.

By 1955 all the buildings in the vicinity of 263 Prinsengracht, including the Annex, were slated to be torn down to make space for an office building. Newspapers mounted a successful campaign to save the Annex, and in 1960 the centuries-old building that housed the Annex opened as the Anne Frank House, a museum devoted to promoting world peace and improved relations among all races. Each year more than six hundred thousand tourists walk through the Secret Annex, which has been restored to the way it looked while Anne and her family hid there. Though Anne's photographs of her favorite movie stars still adorn her bedroom wall, visitors ignore them to learn about a young girl. The movie stars' fame has faded, but the world remembers Anne Frank.

Only three Jewish classmates of Anne's survived the war. Almost nine out of every ten Jewish children alive before World War II died in the Holocaust, and a total of 2 million children of all nations and religions perished in that destructive conflagration. To prevent this from again occurring, the Anne Frank House and its companion organization, the Anne Frank Foundation, host conferences and seminars to spread information about tolerance and understanding.

Anne Frank would have loved the words of Jan Romein, who wrote the article that first gave national attention to the diary. The Dutch historian was so impressed with Anne's gift that he said, "If all the signs do not deceive me, this girl would have become a talented writer had she remained alive." [144]

However, she would have shuddered at another passage from the same article, in which the author concluded,

What matters far more is that her young life was willfully cut short by a system whose witless barbarity we swore never to forget or to forgive while it still raged, but which, now that it belongs to the past, we are already busily, if not forgiving, then forgetting, which ultimately comes to the same thing. [145]

Notes

Chapter 1: "They had Simply Closed the Door of Their Lives"

1. Miep Gies with Alison Leslie Gold, *Anne Frank Remembered: The Story of the Woman Who Helped to Hide the Frank Family*. New York: Simon & Schuster, 1987, pp. 81, 86.

2. Anne Frank, *The Diary of a Young Girl: The Definitive Edition*. Edited by Otto H. Frank and Mirjam Pressler. New York: Doubleday, 1995, p. 19; Netherlands State Institute for War Documentation, *The Diary of Anne Frank: The Critical Edition*. New York: Doubleday, 1989, p. 206.

3. Frank, *The Diary of a Young Girl*, pp. 19–20.

4. Gies, *Anne Frank Remembered*, pp. 87–88.

5. Gies, *Anne Frank Remembered*, pp. 93–94.

6. Gies, *Anne Frank Remembered*, pp. 94–95.

7. Gies, *Anne Frank Remembered*, pp. 94–95.

8. Frank, *The Diary of a Young Girl*, pp. 20–21.

9. Frank, *The Diary of a Young Girl*, p. 20.

10. Gies, *Anne Frank Remembered*, pp. 95–96.

11. Frank, *The Diary of a Young Girl*, p. 21.

12. Frank, *The Diary of a Young Girl*, p. 21.

13. Gies, *Anne Frank Remembered*, pp. 96–97.

14. Gies, *Anne Frank Remembered*, pp. 97–98.

Chapter 2: The Franks in Germany

15. Quoted in Daniel Jonah Goldhagen, *Hitler's Willing Executioners: Ordinary Germans and the Holocaust*. New York: Knopf, 1996, p. 50.

16. Goldhagen, *Hitler's Willing Executioners*, p. 82.

17. Goldhagen, *Hitler's Willing Executioners*, pp. 92–93.

18. Ruud van der Rol and Rian Verhoeven, *Anne Frank: Beyond the Diary*. New York: Viking, 1993, pp. 14–15.

Chapter 3: "The Kind of Child I'd Like to Have"

19. Gies, *Anne Frank Remembered*, p. 32.

20. Gies, *Anne Frank Remembered*, p. 32.

21. Quoted in Willy Lindwer, *The Last Seven Months of Anne Frank*. Translated by Alison Meersschaert. New York: Anchor Books, 1991, pp. 14–15.

22. Quoted in Lindwer, *The Last Seven Months of Anne Frank*, pp. 16–17.

23. Quoted in Jacob Boas, *We Are Witnesses: Five Diaries of Teenagers Who Died in the Holocaust*. New York: Scholastic, 1995, p. 158.

24. Quoted in Lindwer, *The Last Seven Months of Anne Frank*, pp. 15–16.

25. Quoted in Boas, *We Are Witnesses*, p. 175.

26. Gies, *Anne Frank Remembered*, pp. 30–47.

27. Quoted in Helen Strahinich, *The Holocaust: Understanding and Remembering*. Hillside, NJ: Enslow, 1996, p. 14.

28. Quoted in Goldhagen, *Hitler's Willing Executioners*, p. 102.

29. Quoted in Lindwer, *The Last Seven Months of Anne Frank*, p. 13.

Chapter 4: "Our World Was No Longer Ours"

30. Gies, *Anne Frank Remembered*, p. 60.

31. Gies, *Anne Frank Remembered*, p. 64.

32. Gies, *Anne Frank Remembered*, p. 67.

33. Gies, *Anne Frank Remembered*, p. 67.

34. Frank, *The Diary of a Young Girl*, pp. 11–12.

35. Quoted in Richard Amdur, *Anne Frank*. New York: Chelsea House, 1993, p. 39.

36. Gies, *Anne Frank Remembered*, p. 69.

37. Frank, *The Diary of a Young Girl*, pp. 9–10.

38. Frank, *The Diary of a Young Girl*, pp. 3–5.

39. Frank, *The Diary of a Young Girl*, p. 10.

40. Frank, *The Diary of a Young Girl*, pp. 17–18.

41. Quoted in Goldhagen, *Hitler's Willing Executioners*, p. 138.

42. Gies, *Anne Frank Remembered*, p. 93.

43. Gies, *Anne Frank Remembered*, p. 87.

44. Frank, *The Diary of a Young Girl*, p. 12.

45. Gies, *Anne Frank Remembered*, pp. 79–80.

46. Gies, *Anne Frank Remembered*, p. 68.

47. Frank, *The Diary of a Young Girl*, pp. 1–2.

48. Frank, *The Diary of a Young Girl*, p. 6.

49. Frank, *The Diary of a Young Girl*, pp. 6–7.

50. Frank, *The Diary of a Young Girl*, p. 16.

51. Frank, *The Diary of a Young Girl*, p. 18.

Chapter 5: "A Thief Was Safe and a Jew Was Not"

52. Quoted in Lindwer, *The Last Seven Months of Anne Frank*, p. 19.

53. Gies, *Anne Frank Remembered*, pp. 97–98.

54. Gies, *Anne Frank Remembered*, p. 102.

55. Frank, *The Diary of a Young Girl*, pp. 25–26.

56. Quoted in Gies, *Anne Frank Remembered*, pp. 101–102.

57. Gies, *Anne Frank Remembered*, pp. 102–103.

58. Frank, *The Diary of a Young Girl*, p. 29.

59. Frank, *The Diary of a Young Girl*, pp. 27–28.

60. Frank, *The Diary of a Young Girl*, p. 30.

61. Frank, *The Diary of a Young Girl*, pp. 55–56.

62. Gies, *Anne Frank Remembered*, p. 110.

63. Gies, *Anne Frank Remembered*, pp. 117, 123, 128.

64. Gies, *Anne Frank Remembered*, p. 114–15.

65. Frank, *The Diary of a Young Girl*, pp. 32–33, 51, 84–85.

66. Frank, *The Diary of a Young Girl*, pp. 33, 42.

67. Frank, *The Diary of a Young Girl*, pp. 126–28.

68. Frank, *The Diary of a Young Girl*, pp. 32–33.

69. Frank, *The Diary of a Young Girl*, pp. 57–58.

70. Frank, *The Diary of a Young Girl*, pp. 54,

71. Frank, *The Diary of a Young Girl*, pp. 32–33.

72. Gies, *Anne Frank Remembered*, p. 137.

73. Frank, *The Diary of a Young Girl*, pp. 103, 118.

74. Gies, *Anne Frank Remembered*, p. 155.

75. Frank, *The Diary of a Young Girl*, p. 88.

76. Gies, *Anne Frank Remembered*, pp. 155–56.

77. Frank, *The Diary of a Young Girl*, pp. 137–38.

Chapter 6: Crushed Dreams and Cherished Hopes

78. Frank, *The Diary of a Young Girl*, pp. 162–63.

79. Frank, *The Diary of a Young Girl*, pp. 189–92.

80. Frank, *The Diary of a Young Girl*, pp. 246–47, 265–66, 269, 275.

81. Frank, *The Diary of a Young Girl*, pp. 249–50.

82. Frank, *The Diary of a Young Girl*, pp. 60, 158, 207–10.

83. Frank, *The Diary of a Young Girl*, pp. 52, 161.

84. Gies, *Anne Frank Remembered*, p. 151.

85. Gies, *Anne Frank Remembered*, pp. 153–55.

86. Gies, *Anne Frank Remembered*, pp. 150–51.

87. Frank, *The Diary of a Young Girl*, pp. 72–73, 83.

88. Frank, *The Diary of a Young Girl*, pp. 72–73, 149–50.

89. Frank, *The Diary of a Young Girl*, p. 301.

90. Frank, *The Diary of a Young Girl*, p. 310.

91. Frank, *The Diary of a Young Girl*, p. 226.

92. Quoted in van der Rol and Verhoeven, *Anne Frank: Beyond the Diary*, p. 76.

93. Frank, *The Diary of a Young Girl*, pp. 205, 276–77, 281.

94. Frank, *The Diary of a Young Girl*, pp. 276, 323–24.

95. Frank, *The Diary of a Young Girl*, p. 331.

96. Frank, *The Diary of a Young Girl*, pp. 252–62.

97. Frank, *The Diary of a Young Girl*, p. 306.

98. Frank, *The Diary of a Young Girl*, pp. 144–45.

99. Frank, *The Diary of a Young Girl*, pp. 247–48, 287.

100. Frank, *The Diary of a Young Girl*, pp. 263, 305–306.

101. Frank, *The Diary of a Young Girl*, pp. 142, 154.

102. Frank, *The Diary of a Young Girl*, p. 311.

103. Frank, *The Diary of a Young Girl*, p. 319.

104. Frank, *The Diary of a Young Girl*, pp. 263, 328.

105. Frank, *The Diary of a Young Girl*, p. 332.

Chapter 7: "Extermination Was the Objective"

106. Quoted in Amdur, *Anne Frank*, pp. 73–74.

107. Quoted in Gies, *Anne Frank Remembered*, pp. 193–94.

108. Netherlands State Institute for War Documentation, *The Diary of Anne Frank: The Critical Edition*, pp. 21–22.

109. Gies, *Anne Frank Remembered*, p. 197.

110. Quoted in Gies, *Anne Frank Remembered*, p. 196.

111. Quoted in Johanna Hurwitz, *Anne Frank: Life in Hiding.* Philadelphia: The Jewish Publication Society, 1988, p. 40.

112. Gies, *Anne Frank Remembered*, pp. 198–99.

113. Quoted in Amdur, *Anne Frank*, pp. 76–78.

114. Quoted in Lindwer, *The Last Seven Months of Anne Frank*, p. 176.

115. Quoted in Lindwer, *The Last Seven Months of Anne Frank*, p. 53.

116. Quoted in Lindwer, *The Last Seven Months of Anne Frank*, p. 55.

117. Quoted in Lindwer, *The Last Seven Months of Anne Frank*, pp. 56, 148.

118. Quoted in Lindwer, *The Last Seven Months of Anne Frank*, p. 56.

119. Quoted in Lindwer, *The Last Seven Months of Anne Frank*, p. 151.

120. Quoted in Lindwer, *The Last Seven Months of Anne Frank*, p. 59.

121. Quoted in Lindwer, *The Last Seven Months of Anne Frank*, pp. 60, 186.

122. Quoted in Amdur, *Anne Frank*, pp. 80–81.

123. Quoted in Lindwer, *The Last Seven Months of Anne Frank*, pp. 191–92.

124. Quoted in Lindwer, *The Last Seven Months of Anne Frank*, pp. 62, 95.

125. Quoted in Lindwer, *The Last Seven Months of Anne Frank*, pp. 98, 190.

126. Quoted in Lindwer, *The Last Seven Months of Anne Frank*, p. 101.

127. Quoted in Amdur, *Anne Frank*, p. 81.

128. Quoted in Lindwer, *The Last Seven Months of Anne Frank*, p. 153.

129. Quoted in Amdur, *Anne Frank*, p. 83.

Chapter 8: "Now Anne's Voice Would Never Be Lost"

130. Quoted in van der Rol and Verhoeven, *Anne Frank: Beyond the Diary*, p. 100.

131. Quoted in Lindwer, *The Last Seven Months of Anne Frank*, p. 71.

132. Quoted in Lindwer, *The Last Seven Months of Anne Frank*, pp. 27–29.

133. Quoted in Lindwer, *The Last Seven Months of Anne Frank*, p. 104.

134. Quoted in Lindwer, *The Last Seven Months of Anne Frank*, p. 104.

135. Quoted in Gies, *Anne Frank Remembered*, pp. 231–32.

136. Quoted in Lindwer, *The Last Seven Months of Anne Frank*, pp. 83–84.

137. Quoted in Gies, *Anne Frank Remembered*, pp. 234–35.

138. Quoted in Gies, *Anne Frank Remembered*, p. 240.

139. Quoted in Hurwitz, *Anne Frank: Life in Hiding*, pp. 51–52.

140. Gies, *Anne Frank Remembered*, p. 246.

141. Quoted in Amdur, *Anne Frank*, p. 95.

142. Quoted in Amdur, *Anne Frank*, pp. 97–98.

143. Quoted in Amdur, *Anne Frank*, p. 99.

144. Quoted in Janrense Boonstra and Marie-José Rijnders, *Anne Frank House*. Amsterdam: Sdu Uitgeverij Koninginnegracht, 1992, p. 68.

145. Quoted in Netherlands State Institute for War Documentation, *The Diary of Anne Frank: The Critical Edition*, p. 67.

For Further Reading

David A. Adler, *We Remember the Holocaust.* New York: Henry Holt, 1989. A superb account of the Holocaust, based heavily on personal recollections and written for young readers.

Richard Amdur, *Anne Frank.* New York: Chelsea House, 1993. An excellent biography intended for the teenage market.

Susan D. Bachrach, *Tell Them We Remember: The Story of the Holocaust.* Boston: Little, Brown, 1994. Printed in conjunction with the United States Holocaust Memorial Museum, this book supplements informative text with numerous photographs.

Jacob Boas, *We Are Witnesses: Five Diaries of Teenagers Who Died in the Holocaust.* New York: Scholastic, 1995. Gripping accounts of life during the Holocaust, written by five Jewish teenagers who died in the war.

Janrense Boonstra and Marie-José Rijnders, *Anne Frank House.* Amsterdam: Sdu Uitgeverij Koninginnegracht, 1992. Informative book in English about the Anne Frank Museum and the life and times of Anne Frank.

Anne Frank, *The Diary of a Young Girl: The Definitive Edition.* Edited by Otto H. Frank and Mirjam Pressler. New York: Doubleday, 1995. This most recent edition for teenagers of Anne's moving diary includes many of Anne's entries that Otto Frank omitted from the first published version.

Miep Gies with Alison Leslie Gold, *Anne Frank Remembered: The Story of the Woman Who Helped to Hide the Frank Family.* New York: Simon & Schuster, 1987. Packed with superb information that only Miep can provide, this book beautifully complements Anne's diary.

Johanna Hurwitz, *Anne Frank: Life in Hiding.* Philadelphia: The Jewish Publication Society, 1988. Written for upper elementary students, this biography offers a fine introduction to Anne Frank's story.

Willy Lindwer, *The Last Seven Months of Anne Frank.* Translated by Alison Meersschaert. New York: Anchor Books, 1991. Survivors of the Holocaust, each of whom knew Anne Frank or were incarcerated in the same concentration camps as Anne, provide stirring accounts of Anne Frank.

Milton Meltzer, *Never to Forget: The Jews of the Holocaust.* New York: Harper & Row, 1976. Useful recounting for younger readers of the Holocaust's impact on people.

———, *Rescue: The Story of How Gentiles Saved Jews in the Holocaust.* New York: Harper & Row, 1988. The book emphasizes courageous actions of non-Jews during the Holocaust to save their Jewish brethren.

Abraham Resnick, *The Holocaust.* San Diego: Lucent Books, 1991. A well-written history of the Holocaust for teenagers.

Gail B. Stewart, *Hitler's Reich.* San Diego: Lucent Books, 1994. An informative account of life under Hitler's rule, written for the teenage market.

Helen Strahinich, *The Holocaust: Understanding and Remembering*. Hillside, NJ: Enslow, 1996. A basic history of the causes and effects of the Holocaust.

Laura Tyler, *Anne Frank*. Englewood Cliffs, NJ: Silver Burdett Press, 1990. A fine basic biography for young readers.

Ruud van der Rol and Rian Verhoeven, *Anne Frank: Beyond the Diary*. New York: Viking, 1993. A superb photobiography based on photographs and information supplied by the Anne Frank House and by Miep Gies.

Dennis Wepman, *Adolf Hitler*. New York: Chelsea House Publishers, 1985. An informative biography of the German leader for junior high school students.

Works Consulted

Lucy S. Dawidowicz, *The War Against the Jews: 1933–1945*. New York: Bantam Books, 1975. Scholarly account of the Holocaust by a prominent Holocaust historian.

Martin Gilbert, *The Holocaust*. New York: Henry Holt, 1985. One of the best accounts of the Holocaust in recent years.

Daniel Jonah Goldhagen, *Hitler's Willing Executioners: Ordinary Germans and the Holocaust*. New York: Knopf, 1996. A thought-provoking book that examines the role of German citizens in the atrocities of these years.

Nora Levin, *The Holocaust: The Destruction of European Jewry, 1933–1945*. New York: Crowell, 1968. A fine history of the Holocaust.

The Netherlands State Institute for War Documentation, *The Diary of Anne Frank: The Critical Edition*. New York: Doubleday, 1989. This most complete accumulation of official information about Anne Frank contains three versions of the diary: Anne's original words, her own revisions of 1944, and the version edited by Otto Frank, first published in Dutch in 1947.

Michael A. Schuman, *Elie Wiesel: Voice from the Holocaust*. Hillside, NJ: Enslow Publishers, 1994. Excellent biography of a Holocaust survivor who became one of the most brilliant writers of our day.

William L. Shirer, *The Rise and Fall of the Third Reich*. New York: Simon & Schuster, 1960. Still one of the best sources of information about Germany under Nazi rule.

John Toland, *Adolf Hitler*. Garden City, NY: Doubleday, 1976. A readable, complete biography of the German leader.

Interview

"Interview with Fritzie Fritzshall," conducted by the United States Holocaust Memorial Museum, June 27, 1990.

Index

Credits

Photos

Cover photo: AKG London

© AFF/AFS Amsterdam, the Netherlands, 29, 30, 33, 42, 56

AKG London, 14, 20, 39, 43, 45, 46, 48, 60, 81, 82

Central State Archive of Film, Photo and Phonographic Documents, courtesy of USHMM Photo Archives, 72

Corbis-Bettmann, 9, 16

Hungarian National Museum, Photo Archives, courtesy of USHMM Photo Archives, 40

National Archives, 22, 26, 36, 53, 69, 70 (right)

The Simon Wiesenthal Center, 32, 37, 66, 70 (left), 71, 73, 76

Text

Quotations from The Diary of a Young Girl: The Definitive Edition, by Anne Frank; Otto H. Frank and Mirjam Pressler, editors; translated by Susan Massotty, are used by permission of Doubleday, a division of Bantam Doubleday Dell Publishing Group, Inc. Translation copyright © 1995 by Doubleday, a division of Bantam Doubleday Dell Publishing Group, Inc.

About the Author

John F. Wukovits is a junior high school teacher and writer from Trenton, Michigan, who specializes in history and biography. His books include biographies of the World War II commander Admiral Clifton Sprague, Barry Sanders, Vince Lombardi, Tim Allen, John Stockton, Jack Nicklaus, Jesse James, Wyatt Earp, and Butch Cassidy. A graduate of the University of Notre Dame, Wukovits is the father of three daughters—Amy, Julie, and Karen.